NINE SIMPLE LAWS
TO CREATE JOY
AND GRACE

NINE SIMPLE LAWS TO CREATE JOY AND GRACE

A Comprehensive Guide to Manifestation

Sue Hanks Singleton
with Aaron L. Singleton

iUniverse, Inc.
Bloomington

NINE SIMPLE LAWS TO CREATE JOY AND GRACE
A Comprehensive Guide to Manifestation

iUniverse books may be ordered through booksellers or by contacting:

iUniverse
1663 Liberty Drive
Bloomington, IN 47403
www.iuniverse.com
1-800-Authors (1-800-288-4677)

Because of the dynamic nature of the Internet, any web addresses or links contained in this book may have changed since publication and may no longer be valid. The views expressed in this work are solely those of the author and do not necessarily reflect the views of the publisher, and the publisher hereby disclaims any responsibility for them.

Any people depicted in stock imagery provided by Thinkstock are models, and such images are being used for illustrative purposes only.
Certain stock imagery © Thinkstock.

ISBN: 978-1-4759-7886-5 (sc)
ISBN: 978-1-4759-7887-2 (ebk)

Printed in the United States of America

iUniverse rev. date: 03/25/2013

Contents

Praise for *Nine Simple Laws to Create Joy and Grace*

"As a student of the law of attraction, I am thrilled with Sue and Aaron Singleton's powerful new book, *Nine Simple Laws to Create Joy and Grace*. If you want the law of attraction to work better for you, *Nine Simple Laws* is your answer. By providing the missing pieces of the puzzle, the other eight universal laws, the authors describe how to manifest the life you desire. This is the guidebook for the life I have been seeking."

—R. E. Baker, accountant and holistic health practitioner

"Sue and Aaron Singleton's book, *Nine Simple Laws to Create Joy and Grace*, is an insightful jewel and the missing link I have been searching for, which 'reminded' me to always approach my lessons in life equipped with the nine universal laws. This book gave me specific, perceptive details in a simple-to-understand format to restore the inner peace, hope, and joy I longed for. I can now easily create the life I love! Pick up this guide and change your life today! I did!"

—Cheryl Ann Gaglione, Reiki master
and holistic healing practitioner

"I am an avid reader of this genre, yet have never encountered this level of information anywhere. *Nine Simple Laws to Create Joy and Grace* is definitely a runaway best seller filled with wisdom for all. Sue and Aaron have created a user-friendly process to apply these simple laws in a fun and creative way to manifest a life you love and desire."

—Cheryl Labrie, office administrator

"*Nine Simple Laws to Create Joy and Grace* is a great guide to help people achieve the lives they truly desire and to better understand their purposes and the importance of living in accordance with chosen ideals."

—Kari Heistad, consultant

"This process to create joy and grace is easy to understand and implement. The additional Stone Play crystal layouts make it exciting and fun to work with the laws. Give *Nine Simple Laws to Create Joy and Grace* to all your family and friends as a life-changing gift!"

—Cheryl Robertson, accountant and consultant

"With *Nine Simple Laws to Create Joy and Grace*, Sue and Aaron Singleton have gifted us with a treasure trove of loving wisdom on the spiritual underpinnings of the laws of the universe and how to use them to create and maintain a more conscious, fulfilled, and dynamic life."

—Barbara Madding, Bachelor of Science Degree in Education, feng shui practitioner, and change agent

About the Authors

Sue Hanks Singleton, Medical Intuitive, BA, MBA, Certified Master Hypnotherapist, Craniosacral Therapist, Energy of Life Master Therapist and Teacher

An internationally renowned medical intuitive with more than twenty years of hands-on experience, Sue Singleton has performed well over eight thousand medical intuitive readings. Highly sought for her exceptionally detailed and accurate health insights, Sue combines more than forty modalities to facilitate healing and transformation for clients.

In addition to her healing credentials, Sue has earned many degrees, including a bachelor of arts and master of business administration. Prior to working full-time in her healing and teaching practice, she served as a corporate finance officer for a multinational corporation, and she has also worked in several executive positions within the banking industry. In 1990, her near-death experience catapulted Sue into the fantastic journey that led her to her true calling as a healer and teacher.

Aaron L. Singleton, Licensed Massage Therapist, Certified Master Hypnotherapist, Craniosacral Therapist, Energy of Life Master Therapist and Teacher

Aaron Singleton is an inventor, visionary, and the founder of The Energy of Life® integrative and intuitive healing process, which promotes total healing of physical, emotional, and spiritual manifestations of disease by empowering clients to participate in regaining their own health.

Aaron possesses incredible intuitive insight and the ability to manipulate multiple energy frequencies simultaneously. His ability to create healing vortices consistently amazes clients and students.

As a master healer and teacher, Aaron applies his extensive skills in physical and emotional trauma release modalities, such as body restructuring, integrative bodywork/massage, energy healing, hypnotherapy, craniosacral therapy, and acupressure to assist his clients in achieving healthy balance.

A US Army veteran, Aaron was a journeyman welder for the US Department of Defense. He served as a massage instructor at the Cayce-Reilly School of Massotherapy in Virginia Beach, Virginia, prior to relocating his healing practice to New England.

The Way to Balance, LLC

Together, Sue and Aaron Singleton are cofounders of The Way to Balance, LLC, Center for Advanced Healing and Training in Amesbury, Massachusetts. They created The Energy of Life® (EOL™) Root Cause Model and EOL Framework for Evaluating and Resolving Disease and Illness, including a collection of powerful EOL healing and self-empowerment tools, workshops, and articles.

Sue and Aaron are renowned for their success with resolving chronic pain, chronic fatigue, fibromyalgia, migraines, knee/hip/back/neck pain, carpal tunnel syndrome, arthritis, seizures, depression, panic and anxiety disorders, asthma, head/spinal injuries, and much more.

They are currently writing a joint autobiography as well as books on topics such as medical intuition, healing and empowering postures from ancient Egypt, healing and transformation with crystals (Stone Play), and visionary acupressure.

Sue and Aaron Singleton are popular speakers at regional and national conferences on topics of health and holistic healing, intuitive development, and ancient Egypt.

They reside in Massachusetts and enjoy camping, hiking, and fishing with their dog in their free time.

For more information about their center, healing services, products, and training, please visit www.TheWayToBalance.com. A number of their products directly support working with the universal laws, including Law of Grace Rings of Oden™ for meditation, Law of Grace, Law of Abundance and Love and Compassion aromatherapy meditation oils, as well as Stone Play kits with crystal matrix mats and additional layouts for connecting with angels, chakra balancing, reducing stress, etc.

Preface

Aaron and I wrote this book in response to requests from our students in our intuitive development training programs. As we spent part of a module discussing the universal laws, a number of students asked us for more insights on how to apply the laws in their daily lives.

Over two decades ago, two significant events changed my life dramatically. One of them was a near-death experience following a car accident, an event that taught me invaluable insights about the human condition and the bigger meaning of life on earth. In that twilight zone between death and life, I literally saw and came to know *the big picture*. I began to understand *how things work* in the universe and the underpinnings of the universal laws. I learned *why we are here* and that my responsibility from that day forward was to help many people from all walks of life lead happier and healthier lives as a medical intuitive, healer, and teacher. My own reintegration into the earthly existence was not always easy despite the insights I had gained about the universal laws. Translating the *spiritual knowing* into words that others can understand takes a bit of practice. I had no one to turn to for advice. This was happening before others had written books about their near-death experiences, and thus, I felt very different from those around me. My family and friends were initially uncomfortable with the changed me.

As I forged my own way, I found that the first people to believe in me were Harmon and June Bro, who lived with Edgar and Gertrude Cayce for approximately one year as Harmon wrote his doctoral dissertation on Mr. Cayce's intuitive gifts. Edgar Cayce was known as "the sleeping prophet," and he is the most-documented medical intuitive to date. Dr. Bro later published *A Seer Out of Season: The Life of Edgar Cayce* (1989).

The most important person who entered my life and believed in me was my husband, Aaron Singleton. He helped me find the courage to fully heal my past and share my gifts with the world at large.

As Aaron and I live, grow, and work together, our overriding goal is to provide our clients and students with straightforward and effective tools for navigating life.

My primary goal in writing *Nine Simple Laws to Create Joy and Grace* is to share that wisdom with you in a practical, fun, and comprehensive guide for living in harmony with the universal laws. I share personal and client stories (without sharing their real names) to show by example how working with the laws inspires joy and grace, even under duress.

Acknowledgments

First and foremost, we would like to thank the Creator for his/her love that flows through all of us and ignites the universe. Your pure love blesses us to be healers and teachers.

We thank our parents for having brought us into this amazing amusement park we call earth. The adventures have been many, and all of them have helped us become who we are. Both of us can say that some of the most precious gifts our parents have taught us are the ways in which we can be gracious, honest, and generous.

Alyssa Couture, an amazing and gifted young artist, helped us bring the universal laws to life with her whimsical, spiritual creations that grace each chapter.

We extend heartfelt thanks to several people who have extensively proofread and offered valuable suggestions during the process of writing this book. Sue's spiritual sister Cheryl Gaglione spent countless hours poring over the manuscript and brainstorming with Sue to edit the final version.

Barbara Madding tirelessly and lovingly provided insightful edits and became our unofficial line editor during the review process. Her invaluable support has extended into several writing projects.

Patti Andrews's technical expertise is only visible to the readers in the Stone Play™ crystal layouts in this particular book. Stone Play is our unique system of placing ordinary crystals in specific geometric formations to create an energy field conducive to meditation, connecting with angels, or creating the frequency of gratitude, unconditional love, and other universal laws. Patti's keen perceptions and suggestions behind the scenes were crucial to Sue's writing process.

We also wish to thank Ruth Baker, Gwen Hadden, Kari Heistad, Jessica Rose, Cheryl Labrie, Cheryl Robertson, and Christine McKenna for their numerous insights and suggestions as unofficial editors and proofreaders.

We are very grateful to our clients, students, and friends who have offered love and support throughout this entire process.

Introduction

Life happens! In the ebbs and flows of the universe, we seem to find ourselves caught in an onslaught of waves at sea at times. On the other hand, perhaps life to you feels more like a tidal wave. I recently reflected on how long it has taken me to write the final two chapters of *Nine Simple Laws to Create Joy and Grace*. Aaron and I own and operate a busy holistic healing center where we see a full schedule of clients and employ a number of therapists and administrators. We teach a variety of workshop topics, and we manufacture and sell many of our own healing products. We are also speakers at a number of national and regional conferences.

In addition, my elderly parents have lived with us for a long time. Aaron's mother eventually passed away after a series of events, and as the health-care proxy for my two elderly aunts, I helped them both cross over. My aunts' situations developed in tandem with my father's two strokes. This is a partial highlight of just a few of our recent life challenges.

So what have I done in light of my own recent life events?

- I rose above the situations and visualized myself riding the crest of my tidal wave on a surfboard. When one is surfing, it is important to stay focused on the horizon and your goal (the shoreline). We all know there are troughs in between waves, but if we keep looking down into the troughs, that is exactly where we will go. We will not stay on the surfboard very long with a downward view and focus.
- I recognized the nine universal laws are at work, as they always are, and that I would complete writing this book in God's perfect timing.
- I applied discernment and contemplation (meditation and our unique intuitive and integrative healing process, which we named "The Energy of Life®") in order to be clear

on my priorities. We teach The Energy of Life intuitive and healing process to students in workshops, on DVD, and in forthcoming books. Clearly, my family's needs and maintaining our healing center rose to the top of the list. I postponed or eliminated a number of items in my responsibility lists and sought new avenues to delegate more.

- I chose to accept and embrace what *is*, not to fight or feel conflicted with the realities and situations at hand. That included releasing any expectations of family members or friends being open to holistic or alternative healing approaches.

How I Came to Know
the Universal Laws

Throughout the earlier years of my life, challenges ranging from sexual molestation and rape to an abusive long-term relationship and career power struggles often threw me into tailspins. At a certain point, I started thinking, *Life is too hard. There must be a better way. I must be missing something.* I rediscovered some books that I had read as a teenager, including books on reincarnation and the Edgar Cayce material on spirituality. Edgar Cayce was one of the better-known and well-documented psychics and health intuitives to date, and he did intuitive readings on a variety of topics. The concept of spirituality began to give me a sense of a bigger picture about life and the journey of human souls.

Many years ago, my life changed dramatically following two significant events. First, I gained the courage to leave the abusive relationship, and consequently, my personal growth and spiritual journey began in earnest. Later on, as I mentioned in the preface, I had a near-death experience following a car accident. My near-death experience transformed how I viewed the human condition, and it also introduced me to the universal laws and *how things work* in the universe.

Have you ever thought, *I wish there was a guidebook for life. My life would be so much easier if I had a reference guide, a road map, or a how-to guide?*

Do you sometimes feel stuck in a rut? Indecisive? Lonely? Stressed? Overwhelmed? Adrift at sea? Have you lost your zest for life? Are you tired or sick? Does life seem like a struggle?

Have you ever felt that the law of attraction passed over you or that there must be something more to life? Do you yearn for joy in your life? Do you desire inner peace? Do you wonder why you are here on earth? Do you have questions but not know who to ask, or do self-help books fail to address your concerns?

The funny thing is that there *is* a guidebook for life. It has existed for a very, very long time. This instruction manual was created way back when your soul was first born, long before your earthly life began, and before your parents gave you a name.

Do you want to know what is even funnier? Deep inside, there *is* a part of you that already knows about this how-to guide. It has been out of sight and out of mind. Giant piles of laundry, junk, and personal problems have accidentally covered the guidebook.

Artist: Alyssa Couture. © 2012 The Way to Balance®, LLC

The innermost part of you (which we call your soul) contains the hidden guidebook. You became so excited about the adventure of being an individual soul that life on earth became similar to your soul enjoying an amusement park. With so many rides and attractions, it can seem almost overwhelming. Just like an amusement park, some parts (the wacky mirrors) are funny. Some are exhilarating (the flying swings), and some are scary (the haunted house). What exhilarates some people terrifies others. Your soul finds it all very amusing and exhilarating. Your human parts may be a little less sure of that.

Let us take Space Mountain at Disney as an example. Most of us know in our minds that Space Mountain is a large roller coaster ride. Well, there are roller coasters at most amusement parks, yet Space Mountain is very different. People experience the ride in nearly total darkness, and there are lights and sounds that mimic stars, comets, and space flight. When you cannot see the cars or tracks in front of you, you make sudden turns. Stars whiz past you, and all things considered, it is a pretty convincing illusion that you are flying in space. Your soul just loves this. It gobbles up this fun experience as an exciting adventure. What about your human parts? That may depend on who you are and what your human life experiences have been.

When I went on Space Mountain for the first time many years ago, I shared a car with a couple of friends, Kate and Alan. The fourth person with us, Dan, would not set foot anywhere near it, so he just waited outside. I sat in front, and Kate and Alan sat behind me. We took off like a shot, and I was beaming and giggling with exhilaration at all the twists, turns, and sudden free falls. *"I am free! I am flying,"* I yelled. At the same time, Kate and Alan were screaming their lungs out, rather scared at moments, and I would have appreciated some earplugs at that point. Now there is nothing wrong or right with any of those responses. Dan did not want to try the ride. Our friends had scared as well as fun responses, and I was totally blissed out. (It is interesting that this ride preceded my near-death experience from a car accident—the ultimate space mountain ride that catapulted me into becoming a medical intuitive. However, that is another story for another day.)

In a way, I did what many souls have done. My mind did have the analytical data. I knew it was a roller coaster ride in the dark, but I chose to keep the analytical thoughts off to the side for a time and have a convincing and exhilarating ride. Our souls think it is much more fun being in an amusement park when we are not constantly in the mind-set of analytical knowledge, logic, or reason.

Ironically, the illusion is more the flip side of Space Mountain. Analytical thinking is the limiting illusion. The exhilarating ride is the ultimate reality. An amusement park is overwhelming if our *focus* is on panic and fear. On the other hand, an amusement park is fun if our focus is on adventure. This guidebook provides a foundation and focus on the laws, while preserving a sense of whimsy and fun. Everyone chooses his/her unique experience in the amusement park with this broader understanding of "how things work." Because your soul always knows the details of the inherent guidebook and laws on a deeper level, this book will simply help you review and refresh that knowledge.

Let's have some fun! Let us get to the ultimate reality of life's guidebook, *Nine Simple Laws to Create Joy and Grace*. Enjoy the ride!

Artist: Alyssa Couture. © 2012 The Way to Balance, LLC

How to Use This Book

Nine Simple Laws to Create Joy and Grace is for a wide range of people—readers ranging from those new to energy concepts all the way to those experienced in the law of attraction and energy principles. We intentionally write for many accessible layers of understanding. At first glance, we explain the universal laws and principles in a very simple way. Yet the more you work with these laws, the more you will gain a profound sense of how the world works and the better able you will become in applying the synergy of the nine laws to create a life that you love.

We dedicate a chapter to each law, including descriptions, examples, quotations, and artwork. At the end of each chapter, you will find the following:

- exercises designed to enhance your understanding of the law and to help you practice its principles on your own
- a daily affirmation for each law to help you focus on its applications and intricacies
- Stone Play™ crystal layouts that create an energy field conducive to working with each law

Stone Play is an empowering and fun way to work with crystals. You place ordinary crystals in specific geometric formations to enhance your meditation and focus with each law. When you place the specific crystals in the positions shown in each chapter, the layout creates an energy field. For example, in the chapter on the law of gratitude, the Stone Play layout creates the energy frequency of gratitude. By sitting over it in a chair or sitting within the formation's energy field, your cellular structure and DNA reads and absorbs the gratitude frequency, which then enhances or heightens your experience of gratitude. Although this book includes formations specific for the nine universal laws, they are part of a larger collection of layouts we have designed for healing, meditation, connecting with angels, and more.

Although we developed the unique concept of Stone Play, Dr. David R. Hawkins, MD, PhD, evaluated and documented the topic of energy frequencies and levels of consciousness. Dr. Hawkins developed a "map" of the levels of human consciousness (also known as the Scale of Consciousness) that utilizes applied kinesiology (a muscle-testing technique) to document the nonlinear, spiritual realm. The research was scientifically validated and published in Dr. Hawkins's doctoral dissertation titled "Qualitative and Quantitative Analysis and Calibrations of the Level of Human Consciousness." This detailed discussion of the Scale of Consciousness and its significance is outlined in his groundbreaking book *Power vs. Force: The Hidden Determinants of Human Behavior* (1998).

The numbers on the Hawkins's scale represent logarithmic calibrations (measurable vibratory frequencies on a scale that increases to the tenth power) of the levels of human consciousness and their corresponding levels of reality. The numbers themselves are arbitrary; the significance lies in the relationship of one number (or level) to another. (For example, Dr. Hawkins's scale goes from one to one thousand.)

We recommend that you read *Nine Simple Laws to Create Joy and Grace* at least twice. The first time, read it completely to gather an overview and understanding. Then reread the book slowly to learn the ways you can put into practice what we are sharing with you. Spend at least a few weeks with each law. Practice the exercises, crystal layouts, and affirmations on a daily basis. Keep a journal of your experiences with the book and the exercises. You should also record your dreams during this time.

Many of you will gain more each time you repeat *Nine Simple Laws to Create Joy and Grace* and the exercises herein. During subsequent journeys through the material, you can either proceed in the order that we have written the laws or follow your intuition about the order.

Have fun with it, relax, and be playful. It is important to take ourselves lightly; this is your ride in the amusement park we call earth.

In this book, you will notice two voices: "we" means Aaron and Sue, and "I" refers to Sue. Although many of the stories, examples, and illustrations are Sue's, Aaron's contributions as coauthor have been substantial and invaluable. We are a team. Yet, at times we share the same stories from a slightly different perspective.

Please note that we have changed the names of all clients, friends, and family members described in this book in order to protect their privacy. All case histories and examples are true. We have only changed the names.

THE NINE
UNIVERSAL LAWS

To be a man of knowledge one needs to be light and fluid.
—Yaqui Mystic

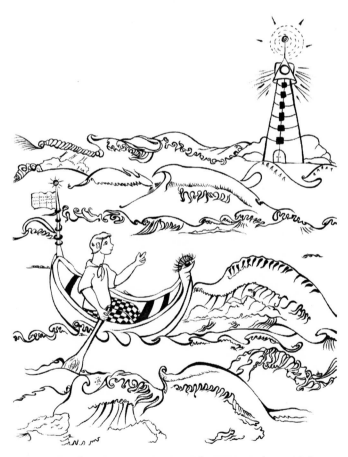

Artist: Alyssa Couture. © 2012 The Way to Balance, LLC

Chapter 1

The Nine Universal Laws

Nine basic "truths" or universal laws operate automatically, whether we are aware of them or not. These laws are not related to religion or religious beliefs. Spiritual and religious beliefs abound, and we respect all of them, as well as each individual's right to choose his or her beliefs. Throughout *Nine Simple Laws to Create Joy and Grace*, we will use the word "God" to refer to "the universe," "universal consciousness," "Creator," or "the One Source." We respectfully ask you to be open to possibilities and word choices.

To keep it simple and straightforward for now, as human beings, we have three aspects that make up the totality of who we are:

1. *Physical body*—the amazing network of bones, muscles, organs, glands, nerves, bodily fluids, etc.
2. *Mind*—our thoughts, beliefs, behaviors, attitudes, memories, and analytical capacities. We can also call this aspect the ego.
3. *Spirit*—the deepest inner essence or spark that is our life force. We call this the soul. It is the miraculous breath of life, the energy of life itself. This spirit aspect is our wise observer within us.

When our souls leave our bodies, our physical bodies become lifeless shells (death). In addition, given the way in which we are defining the term "mind" here, that departs as well.

The nine universal laws apply to and affect our aspects of body, mind, and spirit. Our unresolved emotions also affect all three aspects. Our birthright is that we have *free will*; we have choices and options regarding our bodies, minds, and spirits. At times, it may not seem that way, and we will explain this "feeling" later in *Nine Simple*

Laws to Create Joy and Grace. Yet *we do have free will,* whether or not we choose to exercise it. Free will means we can choose to do the following:

a. Work with the flow of the universe and understand that the universal laws are active.
b. Ignore the laws, even though they impact us all.
c. Work against the laws by trying to battle with them.

Which do you think would be the simplest, smartest way to apply your free will? When we choose (b) or (c) above, we operate in an emergency or survival mode as a direct result. This is also known as *immediate survival instincts*—an existence of chaos, confusion, overwhelming impulses, despair, and rapid swings from one extreme to another.

With this, we tend to find ourselves adrift at sea, and we feel like we are aboard a small boat atop fifteen-foot waves. Without our ocean charts to show us the way home, our boat's operating manual, or our lighthouse beacon to illuminate the right direction, the sea is a very frightening and dangerous place to be. Are you ready to take control of your boat?

The Nine Universal Laws

Here are the nine laws that can assist you in navigating your life with greater ease and joy:

1. The law of divine oneness
2. The law of unconditional love
3. The law of cause and effect (karma)
4. The law of ideals
5. The law of attraction (manifestation)
6. The law of polarity (balance)
7. The law of abundance
8. The law of gratitude
9. The law of grace

All of these laws are operating right now in your life. All of these laws work hand in hand with each other. A helpful metaphor is to imagine that the universal laws represent a team of professionals working on a building project. In this metaphor, some of these laws are *architects with blueprints,* and some are reliable *builders/carpenters* who carry out the architectural plan. Others are *infrastructure specialists* who provide electricity, heat, water, and telecommunications conduits and pathways (e.g., plumbers, electricians, etc.).

It is important that we have all three—architects, builders, and infrastructure specialists—on our team. Would you ever consider building a multilevel home without an architectural blueprint? Would you call up a team of builders and say, "Hey! Come on over to my yard, and let's start a house this weekend"? Would you build the house on the bare ground without some sort of foundational structure or basement? Would you want a house without water, electricity, or heat? Probably not. It would likely be a very crooked, cold, and dark house, one that probably would not withstand a heavy winter or a big windstorm. It would also lack some of the important things that would transform the structure from a house to a *home.*

You really want and need all three types of people on your team. No one is better than the other is. No one is unimportant when you are building a home you will love to live in. This is what it means to work with the laws. You need all of them to work hand in hand in order to build a life you love.

Why Nine Laws?

Some traditions would say there are fewer or more than nine universal laws. From Aaron's and my own experiences, including my near-death insights, we believe that nine is correct. When we pray for clarity or intuit the answer, we consistently receive the answer that there are nine laws, as we have described them. Over the years at various junctures in our lives, we have asked, "What force or law is at work here? What do we need to know?" As our experiences and insights expanded over the years, we decided to summarize and clarify the nine universal laws in this book.

The word "law" is important here. The Encarta online dictionary defines law as: (1) "a binding or enforceable rule"; (2) "divine will" or the principles set forth by the Creator.

A law is not negotiable. A law is enforced. It is the way things work. It is not a trait, attribute, or characteristic that we have or desire to have. Frequently, when someone sets forth a long list of universal or spiritual laws, many traits or attributes are mistakenly listed as laws.

Nine is a very interesting number. It is a "complete number" in that it keeps reproducing itself. No matter what number you multiply it by, the digits add up to nine. For example, 9 x 3 = 27, and 2 + 7 = 9. Or 9 x 9 = 81, and 8 + 1 = 9, and so on. One could say that this trend shows the perfect manifestation of Spirit/God.

In numerology, the number nine has a sense of completeness and divine order. Some consider nine to represent the perfect movement of God. A complete circle is 360 degrees, and its digits (3, 6, and 0) equal nine when added together. Malas (Buddhist prayer beads) have 108 beads (1 + 0 + 8 = 9).

The Bible says there are nine fruits of the spirit, specifically aspects of the Creator, imbued into our human nature. These include love, joy, faithfulness, peace, kindness, long-suffering, goodness, gentleness, and self-control (Galatians 5:22–3 KJV). The Bible further says that there are nine gifts of the Holy Spirit, referencing the ways in which we may choose to manifest our divine nature in human form. These gifts are knowledge, wisdom, faith, miracles, prophecy, discerning of spirits, healing, speaking in tongues, and interpretation of tongues (Romans 12:6–8 NIV, 1 Corinthians 12–14 KJV).

Nine Simple Laws to Create Joy and Grace does not focus on gifts or fruits of the spirit as such, except that some will come into the realm of other tools in chapter 12.

Lastly, the Beatles quite liked the number nine! The song "Revolution 9" from *The White Album* (The Beatles, 1968) kept repeating the phrase, "Number nine." (We could not resist that one for all of us baby boomers.)

Experiential Exercise

Here is something fun to try with our metaphor of the construction team. Without peeking ahead, can you guess which laws are architects, which are infrastructure specialists, and which are carpenters?

In case you need a hint, remember that there are three of each type. If you need a second hint, you should know that they are not necessarily next to each other on the list.

We will explore each of the nine laws in more detail in the following chapters. We reveal the answers to this exercise in chapter 11.

1. The law of divine oneness
2. The law of unconditional love
3. The law of cause and effect (karma)
4. The law of ideals
5. The law of attraction (manifestation)
6. The law of polarity (balance)
7. The law of abundance
8. The law of gratitude
9. The law of grace

THE LAW OF DIVINE ONENESS

"Having pervaded this whole universe with a fragment of Myself, I remain." That is to say, His nature is not exhausted by entering into the various forms of manifestation. That which is able to enter into things yet transcend them must necessarily be abstract. But what is abstract to us need not be unreal. It may be more real than the concrete things we are able to perceive and contact. The Spirit is that which fills the consciousness, whereas matter is only touched by the latter. A vital difference between what we call Matter and what we call Spirit lies in the fact that every element of matter merely brushes the consciousness, whereas when we experience the nature of Spirit in any of its manifestations, it has the quality of filling and pervading the consciousness. [sic]
—Shri Krishna, *Bhagavad Gita*

Artist: Alyssa Couture. © 2012 The Way to Balance, LLC

Chapter 2

The Law of Divine Oneness

Think of the earth as a single planet, with the oceans on the planet as all one giant body of water. The oceans all have unique names and characteristics, but they are all ultimately part of the larger water system. We can also think of the air we breathe as being the same. Because of the spin of the earth, the air molecules circulate without barriers. Technically, we are breathing some of the same air molecules recycled from modern China as well as ancient Egypt.

Another way of perceiving this phenomenon is by remembering a feeling of deep connection you shared with someone or something outside yourself. Aaron explains that when we occasionally watch *Extreme Makeover: Home Edition* on television, we feel incredible empathy for the pain, suffering, and struggles of the family receiving the gift of a home makeover. We are very touched by the sense of community and purpose shared by all who work on the project to change the family's challenging circumstances. Knowing that strangers care about their situation can be very emotional for the family. Aaron says, "We cry almost every time they move that bus." Have you ever cried when they moved that bus? That simultaneous sharing of joy by all the viewers at home, the live participants, and the receiving family is a manifestation of divine oneness.

Although I was aware of this oneness as a young child, I suppressed this knowledge as I got older. I saw tiny moving particles in the air, in plants, and in people. The particles looked the same but organized differently to be a plant or a person. I felt an incredible connection with nature, and my body buzzed with excitement as I connected with my dogs, cats, horses, turtles, and insects. I felt the childlike wonder of being one with my surroundings.

There are truly no boundaries between us. We are ignited and connected by something we all share, namely divine oneness. As the quote from the Bhagavad Gita indicates, the Divine is constant, it remains. Even though spirit pervaded the entire universe with fragments of itself, spirit still *is* (Shri Krishna, 2000). Furthermore, it pervades everything. There is no place that spirit is *not*. It occupies every space in the universe: your body, your car, your house, the plants, animals, your dining room table, and so on.

Moreover, there are parallels, or correspondences, between spirit and the world we all live in. "As above, so below; as below, so above," is one way of stating it. Divine oneness is in the realm of the spiritual and yet affects the physical and mental realms as well. What we do in the physical and mental realms affects the spiritual realm.

In order to grasp the law of divine oneness, we need to understand the concept of *vibration* or *energy*.

Vibration or Energy

Nothing is completely at rest. As humans, we experience material objects as solid. Science, with the advent of electron microscopes, realizes that seemingly solid objects are actually composed of vibrating atoms. Protons, electrons, and neutrons are spinning and moving, never staying still. The space between them allows for movement. The vibratory rate of the atoms is what differentiates whether water is solid (ice), liquid, or gas (steam). Atoms are a manifestation of the divine oneness in the universe.

Imagine our human worldview before electron microscopes. We truly believed that material objects such as rocks were solid and unchanging. We did not *know* that which we did not know at that point in time. Before we knew about vibrating atoms, it was already true that all matter was composed of vibrating matter, not solid and unchanging. We were simply unable to see and know that fact before electron microscopes. This illustration helps us understand that matter is both real and illusory. The physical realm we live in as humans on earth is both real and illusory. There is knowledge that is beyond our comprehension at this point in our human evolution.

Call it a mystery, higher truth, higher intelligence, or perhaps a plan bigger than we can completely know right now.

Everyone and everything in the universe is constantly in motion, growing and changing. Many cells have died, and others have multiplied in the time it took you to read this sentence. As humans, we are moving with the earth as it rotates on its axis at 1,042 miles per hour. At the same time, earth revolves around the sun, traveling at 67,062 miles per hour. Nothing is permanent and unchanging, except the "One Source of All" creating and permeating all that is.

Our human bodies are so amazingly complex that an incredible higher intelligence must have created us. One human eyeball is more intricate than any man-made system to date, containing about 137 million photoreceptors and more than *one billion total parts.* In comparison, NASA's space shuttle Columbia has *only 5.2 million parts.* Most of us would not be able to fully understand the space shuttle or operate it, even though it is simpler than one human eyeball.

Let us call the higher intelligence, the something that pervades all and is the source of all, "divine oneness." We will cover the concept of energy or vibration further in chapter 3, "The Law of Unconditional Love" and chapter 6, "The Law of Attraction (Manifestation)."

A State of "Beingness"

In the very beginning, the Original One Source/God *was all there was.* Nothing else existed. It is a state of "I am," pure "beingness" that is analogous to the sun, meaning all the rays and particles of sunlight that are part of the sun as well as those emanating from it. There is tremendous energy at the core of the sun and in the light rays radiating from it. The power and infinity of the electromagnetic spectrum was not yet obvious.

Another way to imagine "beingness" is to think of a time before our individual souls existed. In the beginning, our core essence was inseparable and fully part of the One Source. We were so entwined as undifferentiated particles that we could not fathom what "I am/ God" was. We were beaming little particles floating around, *"Bliss, bliss, bliss, bliss, bliss—Love, love, love, love, love—"* Perhaps we little particles became bored or curious and wondered, *Who am I? What is "I am"? What is love? Is this all there is?*

Without something to compare One Source with, there was no way of truly knowing God's infinity and power. In a realm of absolutes, where comparison was impossible, something was needed to *experience against* in order for "knowingness" to occur. To know what "is," we must know what is "not." We do not know white without knowing black. Without this ability to compare, we may not even comprehend another option. If you own a black-and-white television and have never seen a color TV, you may not even believe that such a device exists.

This is where One Source recognized that "beingness" needed "experience" in order to complete "knowingness." Thus, free will and individual souls were born. We were given choices to explore different aspects of existence on earth, the great amusement park. In order to truly know love, we need to experience something quite different from it, such as anger or hatred. Some of these extremes help us simply define boundaries or aspects.

How many times were you told as a child, "Don't touch that burner on the stove. It's hot. You'll hurt yourself"? You heard it, but did not truly *get it* until you *experienced* it. Free will is essential for growth and wisdom to occur. No matter how much we would like for our children to avoid anything unpleasant or potentially painful, their free will provides them with invaluable experience. This is how the Creator parents us; we choose our own ways to realize eventually that we are all part of the divine oneness. Within our souls, we are all part of the same family.

The deeper reality is that there is no separation between the One Source and us. Everything is a manifestation of God. We are all a part of the whole and all of our actions affect everyone and everything. Love is a fundamental aspect of what divine oneness is and how it operates in the universe. We will define "love" in chapter 3, "The Law of Unconditional Love."

Exercises for the Law of Divine Oneness

Exercise #1

Imagine or remember a situation, movie, or television show that opened compassion in your heart for someone's pain and suffering. Then remember or imagine how someone or something intervened in this situation. Perhaps you saw an episode of *Extreme Makeover: Home Edition* or *Touched by an Angel,* or maybe you watched an inspiring movie like *War Horse.*

How does it feel to share a deep connection with someone you do not personally know? What is it like to share in their challenges and triumphs?

Exercise #2

Use this exercise to enhance your awareness of your personal connection with the divine oneness as well as to see all individuals as manifestations of divine oneness. We are all one, not separate.

Take a few minutes to find a quiet space to sit or lie down. Imagine, visualize, create, or feel a glowing ball of light in front of you. From this ball of light, imagine radiating lines of light that intersect with each other, much like a big net or a spider web of light or the lines of longitude and latitude around the globe of the earth.

Imagine smaller balls of light at each intersection of the net or web. Each of these represents an individual soul. You may intend that some of these small balls of light represent family members or close friends.

To create a better personal connection with the people represented, see one person as a ball of light. Reach out and bring this ball of light into the center of your chest. Repeat this with additional balls of light.

Notice the intersecting lines lighting up as a communication network among the entire grid. All souls rejoice when we have this type of reconnection. What do you feel or imagine for yourself with this type of soul-to-soul connection?

Exercise #3

Hold a rock, crystal, seashell, or spoon. Look at all its components (color, size, weight, etc.). See how different this object is from you.

Hold the object to your third eye (the lower forehead approximately one inch above the bridge of your nose). Allow the object to join with you and enter your energy field. Use your imagination: What can the rock tell you about itself, its life, or its knowing? What do you wish to tell the object about your perceptions?

Exercise #4

Lean against a tree trunk or float on top of water. Similar to the above exercise, see, feel, or know all its components (firmness, temperature, texture, movement, etc.). Imagine melding your energies with the tree or water. Become one with it. What can the tree tell you about itself, its life, or its knowing? What do you wish to tell the tree about your perceptions?

Affirmation for the Law of Divine Oneness

Speak this affirmation aloud slowly, deliberately and from your heart with feeling: "I am (your name); I am one with the universe. I am fully supported by the natural flow among each and every one of us. We are one in the radiant light of God/the One Source."

Repeat this at least nine times—three times each for your body, your mind, and your spirit. You may repeat this as many times throughout the day as you like. Take five to ten minutes to set a great tone for your daily activities.

We recommend that you use your affirmation with the associated Stone Play crystal layout on page 18, which will enhance your affirmation experience for the law of divine oneness.

This Stone Play layout creates the frequency, or energy, of divine oneness. Sit on a chair over it, lie on a table above it, or sit near it. Be in a quiet, receptive space to experience the frequency of divine oneness. Allow divine oneness to vibrate cellular memory or structure and open you up to more lightness of being.

Pay attention to subtle body sensations, images, or thoughts that come up.

Stone Play Crystal Layout
for the Law of Divine Oneness

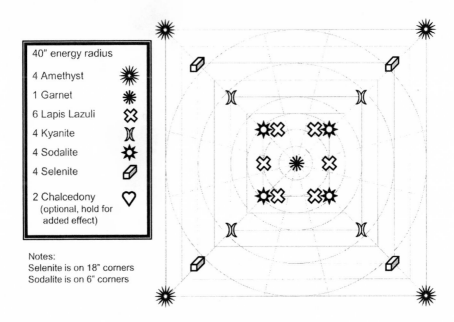

40" energy radius

4 Amethyst	✳
1 Garnet	✳
6 Lapis Lazuli	✕✕
4 Kyanite	)(
4 Sodalite	☀
4 Selenite	▱
2 Chalcedony (optional, hold for added effect)	♡

Notes:
Selenite is on 18" corners
Sodalite is on 6" corners

© 2012 The Way to Balance, LLC

THE LAW OF UNCONDITIONAL LOVE

Your neighbor is your other self dwelling behind a wall. In understanding, all walls shall fall down. Who knows but that your neighbor is your better self, wearing another body? See that you love him as you would love yourself. He too is a manifestation of the Most High.

—Kahlil Gibran, *The Prophet*

Artist: Alyssa Couture. © 2012 The Way to Balance, LLC

Chapter 3

The Law of Unconditional Love

This law pertains to both the self and others, and it is sometimes called the law of acceptance. It is also the law of divine love. It is a state of acceptance, allowing, and nonattachment that forms no emotional cords. It is the practice of noninterference. For ourselves, it involves loving all definable aspects that comprise our total personhood. We have our body, mind, and spirit/soul aspects. To review what we said earlier, the *physical body* is the amazing network of bones, muscles, organs, glands, nerves, bodily fluids, etc. The *mind* includes thoughts, beliefs, behaviors, attitudes, memories, analytical capacities, and emotions. We can also call this aspect the ego. Our *spirits* are our deepest inner essences or sparks that are our life force. This spirit or soul aspect is the wise observer within us. This soul aspect is the part of you that most readily *knows* divine oneness. Unconditional love or divine love is the "soup" we all float in as creations of divine oneness.

Aaron recounts how we experienced unconditional love in connection with a cat:

> Sue and I went to the local SPCA to take an injured baby bird for treatment. Although we had talked about adopting a dog someday, neither of us would have called ourselves "cat people." Much to my surprise, after we handed the baby bird over, I felt compelled to go into the cat room. Sue gave me a very surprised look. As I entered the cat area, I saw a cat inside a large solitary cage on the far side of the room. Before I could even get close enough to look at her, I felt her intense sadness and grief. My eyes welled up with tears, and I felt unconditional love for this beautiful cat. I knew she was

coming home with us. As I approached the cage, she began to stare at me, and I read a sign on the cage. She had been in this cage for nine months, and she was going to be euthanized soon. Sue approached from behind, and she started to cry too.

We spoke with an SPCA employee who told us "Kitty Girl" was in this cage alone because she had tried to kill the other cats in the group room. Her human family had abandoned her. We instantly fell in love with Kitty Girl despite the ridiculous name that conflicted with her regal demeanor and beautiful gray tortoiseshell (tortie) markings. The employees told us she had a nasty disposition. They would prefer that we adopt a pair of cats because we had enough room for two in the house. We humored them and looked at the cat siblings, but we returned to Kitty Girl. They insisted we could not adopt her until we spent time with her in the "get acquainted" room. An employee put on a leather apron and leather gloves and carried a big towel to Kitty Girl's cage. As soon as she opened the cage, Kitty Girl hissed, clawed, and bit the employee's leathered hands and arms. She wrestled with her and closed the three of us into the glass-walled "get acquainted" room. We felt nothing but intense unconditional love for this sad and abandoned cat as she hissed, spit, and snarled at us. After about fifteen minutes, Sue went to the front desk and requested to proceed with the adoption. The employees were shocked and asked, "Are you sure?" Sue replied that all Kitty Girl needed was a loving home and a healing of her abandonment issues.

They placed Kitty Girl (still hissing and clawing vigorously) into a pet carrier, and we were on our way home. Sue and I both talked to her as she wailed loudly, trying to comfort and assure her that she was safe and loved. Kitty Girl told Sue, "You have got to give me a more royal name. No more of this Kitty Girl crap!" I guess she was pretty opinionated. (And I'm sure you noticed that we can talk to animals.) At home, we closed her in our bedroom to begin creating a larger safe place than a cage for her. Sue asked her what kind of name she wanted. Kitty Girl responded that she wanted an Egyptian name. "And if it doesn't have Ra (the

Egyptian sun god) in it, I won't answer to it." Boy did we love this feisty cat! Given that Ra was masculine, we scanned through a list of Egyptian god and goddess names. Sue found "Shait," which was the female goddess that helped evaluate what a person had done wrong or right after the person crossed into the afterlife. Perfect fit. Therefore, we named her Ra-Shait. Sue called out her new name, and Ra-Shait came running to us like a puppy dog. Yet if we tried to pet her or pick her up, she clawed and bit us. Still, we loved this cat. She began sleeping on our bed with us the very first night. It took some time before we could freely pet her and pick her up. We still have our beautiful Ra-Shait, who is now twenty-one years old. She continues to be opinionated, but she is also a very loving and sweet cat. We learned how unconditional love could heal.

I remember working with a client named Cynthia who had significant anger issues. She was a professional interviewer and television show host. Session after session, she would come in and tell me how awful her parents were when she was growing up, and she blamed anyone and everything around her for her situation in life. She was miserable, lonely, and unhappy. She drove her friends away. I would perform a series of healing techniques, energy work, emotional release from the body, and hypnotherapy for her. I would ask her questions about her conclusions that everyone else was to blame, about how it was never her fault. One day, something I asked or said obviously triggered Cynthia. She raged, swore at me, and called me unrepeatable names. I gave her space because I knew it was not truly personal, and I kept beaming unconditional love to her. The blaming and yelling went on. I found it rather challenging to stay in this loving space, and yet I did. About fifteen minutes into her rage, Cynthia suddenly burst into tears and said, "Oh, my God! It isn't you at all. You aren't all those things I just said. It's *me*." I hugged her as she sobbed. I told her I loved her. She was shocked. "How can you love me when I just yelled at you and called you horrible names?"

I replied, "My love is unconditional. It is not based on what you say or do. I love you for being your authentic self." I guided Cynthia through some self-forgiveness exercises. By the end of the session, she was a changed woman. The harsh edge was gone, and she had a glow about her. She continued to express her gratitude for years to come. It was such a powerful turning point in her life that she changed the focus of her professional interviews and television shows. She gained new friends and healed old friendships.

We understand from the prior chapter that divine oneness creates and permeates everything that exists and that it relates to energy, vibration, and movement. However, how does the Creator do this? What is the energy of creation and life as we know it? The energy of creation is the adamantine particle: the smallest, most elemental particle in the universe, smaller than a quark, smaller than any subatomic particle recognized by science. It is a minute, indivisible particle of light that is the building block of all matter, the element necessary to create everything that exists in the universe. The adamantine particle is the core building block to the thought forms your brain generates, as when you imagine or visualize something.

The adamantine particle is the divine spark of creation. What the particle *becomes* changes form according to how it is organized and how fast it vibrates. Adamantine particles are the building blocks of your liver as well as the maple tree planted in the yard. The particle itself is composed of both matter and antimatter and may be experienced as both particles and waves. It may be unfathomed thus far by Western science. As of 2012, scientists working with the Large Hadron Collider (LHC) in Geneva, Switzerland, believe they may have found this "God particle." The scientists refer to it as the Higgs boson of the standard model.

By various names, the God particle has been recognized by numerous ancient spiritual practices, including ancient Chinese and Hindu traditions and perhaps known by Jesus (back before science and spirituality were separate concepts). This name we have provided, adamantine particles, first became apparent to us via Glenda Green's book *Love without End* (1999), which helped us put into words how we do our healing work. This book is the remarkable story of an artist whose landscape paintings hang at the Smithsonian Institution in Washington, DC, and her unexpected encounter with Jesus. He manifested physically and appeared in her artist studio for a series of sittings during which Glenda painted his portrait. During these meetings, Glenda and Jesus talked about a whole range of topics, and he answered her many questions about science, spirituality, and more. Prior to these encounters, Glenda described herself as not particularly religious or spiritual. The book is the result of the extensive notes she took during these personal visits.

When Glenda Green asked Jesus to define adamantine particles, he replied, "They are the fundamental building blocks of physical existence. They are particularized energy potentials which activate, unify and give form to infinity." He continued, "One way of stating it is that they are the ultimate points which unify infinity and activate its potential" (Green, 1999).

When Glenda said, "How could infinity be unified? That seems like an oxymoron," Jesus replied, "I'm sure it does from the point of view you are using to explain the physical plane. Right now, human understanding of energy and matter is limited by the concept of energy as force. Most of science and most thinking interpret energy as force, combustion and pressure waves. The [current human] concept goes something like this. Force results in pressure waves, pressure waves create density, density results in matter [*active component*], and everything left over is infinity [*passive component*]. That is the oxymoron!"

Current human understanding cannot truly grasp infinity. Jesus concludes, "A leftover cannot be defined and provides no basis for interaction. As long as [humans regard infinity] as an indefinable leftover, how can its properties be described [to a human being]?" (Green, 1999).

Even some modern scientists tend to have a broader understanding of the concept of energy exchanges and the *unseen* forces at work, although they do not use the term adamantine particle. One is Dr. Bruce Lipton, world-renowned American cell biologist who proved that thoughts could change tissue samples in a petri dish (Lipton, 2008). Another is Dr. Fritz-Albert Popp, the groundbreaking German biophysicist who scientifically proved we are indeed *beings of light* emitting light photons continuously.

Infinity is not a leftover at all. As long as humans define energy as force, we will not fully comprehend adamantine particles. Nor will we be able to travel to faraway galaxies. The non-force component of adamantine particles is magnetic, not in the sense of magnets as we currently know them but as an aspect of the Creator called unconditional love, the Holy Spirit, and the Energy of Life. It is the divine spark that creates and permeates *all that is*. We will further this discussion with yin/yang and balance concepts in chapter 7, "The Law of Polarity (Balance)."

To practice the law of unconditional love, give yourself permission to sit back and create some space around your soul/spirit, mind, and body aspects. Recognize that each part of you has a unique experience and way of operating. Think of your soul as your wise observer patiently *seeing* without reacting.

Imagine looking outside and seeing a streetlight. Look at its location and its purpose. Do you have an emotional attachment to the streetlight or to its location or purpose? Probably not. However, if you do (perhaps it shines in your face as you are trying to fall asleep at night), will yelling or complaining at the streetlight change its location or purpose? Can you simply observe the light and accept it exactly as it is? In order to practice the law of unconditional love, you must practice allowing yourself to observe and accept yourself and other people much in the same way you accept the streetlight.

In doing this, we observe in a nonjudgmental manner. We simply allow others and ourselves to be exactly as we are. That is what the Creator does for us. The Creator gives us space to be exactly who we are. We can choose differently based on what we learn from our current or past situations. We can adapt. For example, perhaps you reposition your bed so the light does not shine in your face, or you can always put up a window shade. The same principle applies to what we observe in others' lives. We can choose to act differently than they do without trying to change them or negate their free will. As you remember from the law of divine oneness, you'll note that God gave each of us free will.

Our souls hold a state of perfection and love that is the very essence of who we are. We *are* love itself manifested into individual life forms. Naturally, we must practice this unconditional love with ourselves first in order to practice it successfully with others. If we do not love ourselves as unconditionally as the Creator does, then we are not truly practicing unconditional love with others. Glenda Green's way of stating this is as follows: "Be the love that you are" (1999).

The Creator loves us exactly as we are. Yet, he loves us so much that he desires that we love ourselves enough to strive to become even better, more fulfilled in life. If we all stand together outside in sunshine, the sunshine reaches every one of us. However, if you choose to step under a tree or inside a building, you may have the misimpression that the sun is not shining. Does the sun actually go away when it is raining? Does it die every night when there is darkness? Of course not. It is always there, even when we cannot see it directly.

Some people are so busy trying to love and help everyone that they do not practice the art of loving themselves through self-care. Self-care and loving yourself is actually a requirement for truly being the best helper and best example of love that you can be. When you fly on an airplane, one of the first things the flight attendants tell you is to "please put on your own oxygen mask first before you try to help others." Self-sacrifice, particularly putting yourself last, ultimately leads to more people *down* and needing rescue. There is always someone in crisis. I know this firsthand as a medical intuitive and healer. With so many people in need, if I had chosen to react to each person in crisis, I would have ignored my own self-care. That means I would probably not be on the earthly plane anymore. Thus, I would not be helping anyone (at least not in the physical, human form).

The law of unconditional love is sometimes hard to grasp when we view it out of context from the other laws, particularly the law of polarity (balance) and the law of cause and effect (karma). It can be especially challenging when we witness parents dying and leaving young children, starvation and disease in many parts of the world, war and terrorism, and/or the death of children.

In the chapter on the law of divine oneness, we said that our *knowingness* is only complete when we combine *beingness* with *experience*. You heard the warning of the hot burner on the stove, knew it conceptually, but did not truly *get it* until you experienced the burn. Chances are you did not put your hand on the hot burner a second time.

If we recognize that each of us has a soul and many experiences to gain, we start to see the bigger picture of the divine plan if we want to complete the equation *beingness + experience = knowingness*.

The unconditional love of the Creator granted us the free will to have experiences and thus truly know what love is. How do we know what love is unless we experience something to compare or contrast with love? We grow to *know* what love is by having experiences that appear to lack love, or by losing love. The irony is that when it feels like our hearts are breaking, that experience affords us the opportunity to open our hearts to deeper levels of knowing love. This relates back to the example of earth being a giant amusement park for our souls. There are many rides and attractions, some fun and some scary. Yet if we get in line for the same ride repeatedly, we have no idea what an amusement park is. We only know one ride. God so loves us that he gave us free passes to the amusement park and opportunities to know it all.

To take this another step further, the universe and the divine plan are efficient and recycling. Does an efficient and recycling universe really create all these souls to live one lifetime of eighty years or so and then shelve them all somewhere? If so, then every new life is a brand new soul. Moreover, the wisdom that those other souls learned will never be shared. If that is true, then it is analogous to withholding generational knowledge and one generation *not* teaching the next what they know. We believe God has a much bigger plan. The Creator is not so wasteful or shortsighted. So little time, so much to learn and know—

Let us suppose for a moment that perhaps our souls do recycle through a multitude of experiences as different people, family choices, religions, ethnicities, cultures, etc. The master plan makes sense. In order to complete our *knowingness*, we need *many* experiences, and these choices are based on our soul's concept of free will and choice. Like actors playing roles on a stage or in a movie, our souls put on various costumes and fully engage in the current roles, as they have for past roles.

In the movie *Silence of the Lambs*, Anthony Hopkins's portrayal of Dr. Hannibal Lecter was very convincing and frightening. Yet, does the actor's decision to accept and play that movie role mean that Anthony Hopkins himself is evil and sadistic? No, it does not. Our souls play a variety of roles over time. As we observe terrorism and war, our human aspect does not know what each soul's experience was prior to the current situation. Over the expanse of time and lifetimes, we all have taken turns being the aggressors and the victims to various degrees. It is very challenging to be an impartial observer to someone being victimized. Yet the next law, that of cause and effect, is another important part of the *law and order* in the universe. It is important to recognize that all of these nine universal laws work together as a team. We are only at the second law right now.

Love is not a romantic notion. Nor is it just an emotion. Love is the power and master plan that makes up all of existence: people, mother earth, plants, animals, rocks, etc. Sometimes love means *tough love* and standing as a mirror and providing strength for someone else. People who have decided to do interventions for family members who are addicted understand that tough love is the right thing, even though it may be hard for the addicted one to see it that way at the time. Yet it is still the loving, right thing to do in certain circumstances.

A very powerful example of this unconditional love can be found in a religious story. A woman who was greatly disfigured from leprosy approached Jesus, tugged at his sleeve, and said, "Heal me . . . *now.*"

He looked directly into her eyes and asked, "Tell me, sister. What have you learned from your condition?"

She angrily replied, "It has taught me that I hate to be ugly! So *make me beautiful*, Master."

With compassionate love and power, he continued looking into her eyes and said, "Obviously, your illness still serves you. I cannot help you." He turned and walked on his way. Her *knowingness* was not complete. She had not fully learned from her *experience.* If he had taken away that experience, she would have to learn it another way, perhaps even a harder way.

The law of unconditional love as well as the law of divine oneness and the law of grace are the result of living in oneness with the Creator. By living in this way, we are supporting the bigger master plan we may not yet fully comprehend. In addition, the people interacting with us may *not* always view our statements and actions out of love in that way. Whether or not others recognize this, that is okay as long as we base our intentions on love and we do not control them or try to force our own personal agendas.

Exercises for the Law of Unconditional Love

Exercise #1

Try to imagine or remember a time when you loved or held a baby or a pet. Feel, imagine, or visualize holding, hugging, rocking, or loving this beautiful baby or pet. Imagine a warm feeling in your chest or heart as you do so.

Imagine this baby or pet has a sore toe. Imagine comforting the sore toe. Perhaps he or she welcomes the comforting. On the other hand, maybe the toe hurts so much that he or she screams or bites you when you try to help.

Are you able to maintain the warm, loving feelings? Remember that the baby or the pet does not realize you are trying to help. Try not to judge him or her. Simply observe and exist in this loving space. Bring this loving feeling toward yourself and into your heart. *Become* unconditional love.

Exercise #2

If feeling love is not possible for you right now, then simply imagine lying down in the warm sunshine in springtime after a long winter. The sun's warm rays penetrate your skin and your chest and create a tingly, warm sensation. Allow a pleasant feeling to flow into your heart and radiate throughout your body. Set the intention that the tingly warmth is your *current* representation of *love*. Loving yourself is the *first* step.

Exercise #3

Practice meditation. Quiet yourself. Smile at each organ. Smile at your teeth, nose, and body parts. Send smiles on every out breath to wherever they are needed or wanted. What is this like? How do your organs respond to this loving smile? How do you feel about yourself?

Affirmation for the Law of Unconditional Love

Speak this affirmation aloud slowly and deliberately from your heart with feeling: "I am as I was created. I am love. I love others and myself. I allow myself to be a wise and compassionate observer of myself and others."

Repeat this at least nine times—three times each for your body, your mind, and your spirit. You may repeat this as many times throughout the day as you like. Take five to ten minutes to set a great tone for your daily activities.

We recommend that you use your affirmation with the associated Stone Play crystal layout on the following page, which will enhance your affirmation experience for the law of unconditional love.

This Stone Play layout creates the frequency or energy of unconditional love. Sit on a chair over it, lie on a table above it, or sit near it. Be in a quiet, receptive space to experience the energy frequency of unconditional love. Allow it to vibrate cellular memory or structure to open you up to more lightness of being.

Pay attention to subtle body sensations, images, or thoughts that come up.

Stone Play Crystal Layout
for the Law of Unconditional Love

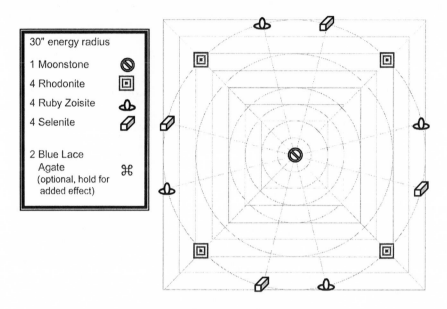

30" energy radius

1 Moonstone

4 Rhodonite

4 Ruby Zoisite

4 Selenite

2 Blue Lace
  Agate
  (optional, hold for
  added effect)

THE LAW OF CAUSE AND EFFECT

Humankind has not woven the web of life: we are but one thread within it. Whatever we do to the web, we do to ourselves. All things are bound together.
—Chief Seattle, Suquamish

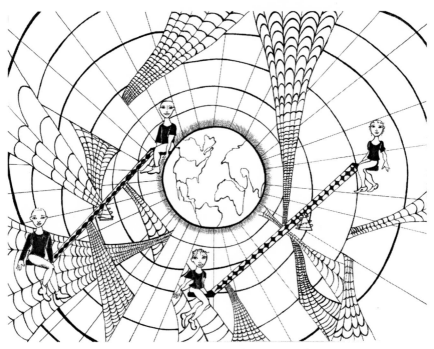

Artist: Alyssa Couture. © 2012 The Way to Balance, LLC

Chapter 4

The Law of Cause and Effect

This law is also called the law of karma. It is a powerful law for teaching us responsibility and accountability for our actions. For every action, there is a reaction. This is similar to the law of physics. The effects of our words and actions come back to us in time, whether in this lifetime or another. Whatever we give, we will receive. These principles are clearly stated in some very commonly repeated phrases: "An eye for an eye, a tooth for a tooth," and "What goes around comes around." If we plant a turnip seed, then a turnip plant sprouts, not an oak tree. If we plant a seed of hatred, then the sprouted plant will also be hatred, not love. There are various levels to this law.

We can view karma on a soul level as well as a human level. If you are cruel and insulting to others, they are very likely to either reciprocate in kind or exit the friendship. If you do not pay your electric bill, the electric company will turn off your electricity. If you do not follow instructions for proper usage of a product, you will void the warranty. If you consistently eat a lot of starches and sugars, you will gain weight and may eventually develop diabetes. At times, the effects of karma are swift, and it is easy to see the connection. At other times, it may take a while for the cause to show its effect.

Examples of the law of cause and effect are evident in our healing work. We frequently trace health issues back to their *root causes*, help the client resolve the cause, and enable a changed effect to restore health.

One example is Jane, a fifty-six-year-old woman who came to us for help with her painful arthritic hands (her *effect*). We found the *cause* was unresolved fear/terror stuck in her hands. At age six, some older kids chased her with a dead animal. Frightened, Jane ran and hid under a porch, cringing and holding her hands tightly in fists.

During this healing session as an adult, she realized that she frequently awoke in the middle of the night, hands tight in fists near her face, feeling an *unknown* fright. Suddenly, she now knew why and knew that it was also the cause of her arthritis. We helped Jane release the fear stuck in her hands, and her arthritis pain went away completely.

Another example is Jim, an eighty-year-old man who came to our center with headaches, dizziness, and motion sickness. We discovered that the cause was physical trauma residues from a time when someone hit him in the head with a brick at age twelve. We used a variety of techniques to remove the trauma, and we then resolved Jim's condition.

Sometimes the causes of our attitudes today are things that we were told as children that we still believe today. Tim, a client whose father died when he was young, spontaneously remembered during a healing session something his uncle had told him at the funeral. "Big boys don't cry. Timmy, you are the man of the house now, so you have to be tough." In a flood of emotion, the adult Tim realized he had been living his life like an emotionless robot, void of all feelings. Even as he suppressed his grief, he suppressed his capacity for joy. This was a beautiful turning point in Tim's life as he gave himself permission to experience both pleasant and uncomfortable emotions. He realized that his uncle's intentions were good but that he could now choose to believe differently than his uncle did. Tim also learned what joy felt like.

Mary was a client on whom I performed a medical intuitive reading by phone. She was looking for help during a challenging pregnancy. She was beginning to show medical signs of rejecting her unborn baby. She was quite far along in the pregnancy and needed to know why and whether the problem could be resolved or not. Much to her surprise, I found that a primary cause of this condition was the result of karma, because as a man in a past life in ancient Greece, Mary had stabbed and killed a pregnant woman and her unborn child. This was unresolved guilt and the law of cause and effect coming into play. Mary burst into tears over the phone and exclaimed, "This is so amazing and strange all at once. I had an emergency appendectomy earlier during this pregnancy. I see the karmic effect so clearly. So why didn't I die under the knife like I did to someone else in another?" I answered her personal questions and explained the karmic concepts that follow.

This law is not a punishment; it is natural cause and effect. Nothing truly happens by accident. Everything has a cause. Think of causes as catalysts in a stream of events, catalysts usually driven by fundamental beliefs about life. Did you learn that the world is an unsafe place as a child? On the other hand, did you learn that people are intrinsically good?

There is positive karma too, also known as the law of good works. It can sometimes totally cancel out bad karma as it did for the client described above. She realized that her *good works* had balanced her karma and fully forgave herself. The medical crisis totally resolved without any medical intervention, and she gave birth to a healthy baby. Simply by working through the karma and ensuing emotions (that her conscious self was not aware of until our session), her body was able to carry the baby to full term with no problems of rejection.

At first, working with the law of cause and effect may cause you to speak and act kindly because you expect something good in return. Sometimes in personal relationships, you may do something you do not want to do simply because you want a reward for doing it. Although this level of cause and effect works, do not stop there. Thus far, you have learned that you have a level of power. Your thoughts, words, and actions have an effect on the world and the people around you. You begin to attract to you people and experiences that are similar to what you give out.

If we do not do this with the right intent, then we are building karmic lessons. For example, most people know individuals who donate their time or money to charitable causes with the agenda of gaining recognition or favors in return. Others may know someone who does a nice deed for a friend and then waits for the friend to reciprocate. If the primary motive of someone's actions is to make a lot of money ruthlessly without caring about other people, there will be an eventual karmic adjustment. Staying at this base level of the law prevents someone from creating positive karma.

Once you work at the base level of the law, you observe the results of cause and effect, and you may not like some of the effects. You can then choose to move to the next level. The higher level of the law of cause and effect is called "responsibility and right action," which leads us to responsibility, right action, and care in our increased sense of power. The law of good works can sometimes activate the law of grace. This is where we learn to release our expectations of rewards. Our motivation is to *do the right thing for the sake of doing the right thing*, not out of the expectation of a reward.

We build our own belief systems. Whatever we believe, say, or do *creates* our reality. We will see our reality as truth. Every cause has its effect and vice versa. We become masters of our own lives when we become conscious *causes* of the *effects* we desire rather than allow others to sweep us along by their wills, desires, or beliefs. When we are able to do this, we cease to be victims or pawns. Instead, we are in charge of our own life choices. Thus, we begin to work consciously with the law of attraction, which we will cover in chapter 6.

Exercises for the Law of Cause and Effect

Exercise #1

Reflect on a situation where you said or did something about which you later did not feel good. Perhaps you did something out of anger or resentment toward someone. For example, you may have yelled at your mother or child, stole from someone, told a lie about someone, lied in order to get a job, cheated on a test, etc.

As you remember it now, what do you notice in your body? Do you feel tense, tight, or stressed? Do you have a stomachache?

Now engage the "wise observer" aspect of yourself (from the law of unconditional love). Without judging yourself, reflect on what happened *because* of what you said or did. How did other people respond? What was the rest of your day or week like?

Next, think of a situation where you said or did something about which you felt very good. Perhaps you gave encouragement or a kind word to a friend or helped someone in need. For example, you may have given five dollars to a homeless person, complimented a friend on a job well done, cooked a meal and taken it to a family in need, etc.

As you remember it now, what do you notice in your body? Do you feel happy, warm, relaxed, or positive? Engage your wise observer again. Without ego or judgment, what happened after you did something nice? How did the other person respond? What was the rest of your day or week like?

What might you learn from comparing these two experiences? Which experience feels better within you? Which would you prefer in your life?

Exercise #2

Reflect on an attitude or belief system you have that you would like to improve or change. For example, maybe you tend to expect the worst to happen, creating a negative outlook. Perhaps you engage in gossip or are overly critical of others. Allow yourself to engage your wise observer and ask to see or know the *cause* of this belief. In a nonjudgmental way, ask yourself, "*Who* did I learn this from? Did I learn it from my parents, grandparents, or other family members? *What event* or circumstance triggered this belief? *Why* do I believe this?"

Once you have done this, imagine how you might feel without this attitude. What might happen if you realized you have a right to believe or speak differently than this other person? What if he or she made a mistake or was incorrect? What if your interpretation of that person or event is not very accurate? Imagine that you have a right to disentangle the historical event from your present *feelings* about it. It could be very freeing to let go of that ball and chain that has been weighing you down.

Affirmation for the Law of Cause and Effect

Speak this affirmation aloud slowly and deliberately from your heart with feeling: "I harvest what I plant in my daily life. I choose to plant beautiful seeds with my thoughts, words, and actions today."

Repeat this at least nine times—three times each for your body, your mind, and your spirit. You may repeat this as many times throughout the day as you like. Take five to ten minutes to set a great tone for your daily activities.

We recommend that you use your affirmation with the associated Stone Play crystal layout on the following page, which will enhance your affirmation experience for the law of cause and effect.

This Stone Play layout creates the frequency or energy conducive to understanding cause and effect. Sit on a chair over it, lie on a table above it, or sit near it. Be in a quiet, receptive space to experience that frequency. Allow it to vibrate cellular memory or structure to open you up to more lightness of being.

Pay attention to subtle body sensations, images, or thoughts that come up.

Stone Play Crystal Layout
for the Law of Cause and Effect

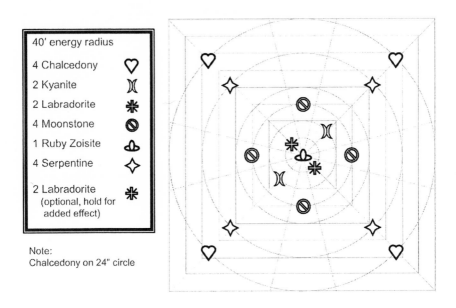

40' energy radius

4 Chalcedony ♡

2 Kyanite)(

2 Labradorite ✳

4 Moonstone ◎

1 Ruby Zoisite ♣

4 Serpentine ◇

2 Labradorite ✳
(optional, hold for
added effect)

Note:
Chalcedony on 24" circle

© 2012 The Way to Balance, LLC

LAW OF IDEALS

Life isn't about finding yourself. Life is about creating yourself.
—George Bernard Shaw

Artist: Alyssa Couture. © 2012 The Way to Balance, LLC

Chapter 5

The Law of Ideals

At first, the George Bernard Shaw quote for the law of ideals may seem like an oxymoron. Yet finding the innermost aspect of yourself is unconditional love, as we just learned in chapter 3. Therefore, once you fully know that you *are* unconditional love, the journey is about what you choose to *create* with the love that you are.

The law of ideals is at work, and you may have an *unconscious* purpose to your life that is contradicting your *conscious* mission in life. On the other hand, maybe you have never noticed that your activities and decisions cancel out what you say your goals are. Your self-talk, favorite phrases, attitudes, and beliefs are always telling the universe what your goals are. How you spend your time, energy, and money tells the universe what you value most. Do you like where you are? Do you find yourself not achieving your goals?

As an illustration of the contradiction between your life purpose and your current activities, ask yourself, "Would I take a trip across the country without any idea about where I was going?" If you hurry to the airport and get on the next flight out of town, you may end up in Atlanta when you intended to travel to Montreal. When you are taking a trip, you probably look at a map and gather some directions to help you reach your destination more easily. Alternatively, if you are out on the ocean in a boat after dark, you will likely look for a lighthouse beacon to guide you to shore.

Living life without clearly defined goals (or ideals) is very analogous to being adrift at sea, tossed by the waves, carried by the prevailing winds and currents. Often, being adrift and lost makes us feel powerless, and we may go into survival mode. We may feel sick and dizzy as we look down at the waves and struggle to catch fish and obtain fresh drinking water. Finding yourself in this situation would be less likely if you had prepared according to well-articulated ideals and goals that were in alignment with your activities. It is not too late to sit back and observe your current situation in order to determine your short-term and long-term goals, to assure that they complement each other.

The first step is to look up and scan the horizon from your boat adrift at sea. Is there a body of land nearby? Is there a boat nearby? Get a sense of north, south, east, and west from what you observe and know or get a map. What is your goal? Your goal is to return to shore safely and come home to loved ones. You may even realize that you are much closer to shore than you had first thought. Now that the rain and waves have calmed, you can get there on your own. On the other hand, you may spot a nearby boat and signal for help.

What is important to realize is that by having a plan, there is no need to panic. Panic does not help your situation. In fact, it probably makes it worse. Do you really want to go home? Why? Who or what awaits you? Assuming you have a pleasant reason to get to shore, imagine yourself happy and relieved, reunited with those you love. After a pretty short time of setting your ideal and focusing on it, you are likely to find a solution or the next step toward the discovery of a solution.

The law of ideals is also called the law of intention. When we have clarity of intention and work with the law of ideals for the highest good, it is easy to make decisions. It also invites the support of the universe via the law of manifestation (attraction). For a second example, you might recognize that the water is cold and that you are far from shore. Given the fact that your goal is to return safely to loved ones, your wise choice is to stay in the boat, create a shelter to protect you from the sun and rain, and ration your food and water supplies. You will also locate or create a receptacle to collect fresh rainwater and create a fishing line and hook. Given your clear goal to return safely to shore, you would not likely decide to jump in the frigid water and start swimming because you know about hypothermia and exhaustion. You will take action steps that positively support your goal to reach the shore safely. You are not likely to swim away from shore if your goal is to return home.

Let us apply this concept to your daily life. If your goal in life is *joy*, then you need to examine what you are doing to support joy in your life. If you choose to spend a lot of time with people who belittle you or who focus on the negative things in life, then you are not supporting your ideal of joy. On some level, you are sharing their misery goal if you choose to stay there. It is important to remember that it is not about where you begin the journey but about where you want to go. There are incredible examples of children whose parents were drug addicts or who lived in homeless shelters with their parent(s), but the kids knew they wanted better lives for themselves. They went to school. They studied, and they chose not to hang out on the streets and get into fights. Despite the environment these children were in, they focused on their positive goals for better lives.

In the movie *The Pursuit of Happyness* [sic], the real characters' ideals helped them stay on a healthier path. Will Smith portrays the real-life person Chris Gardner, who was formerly homeless but then became a millionaire. He and his young son struggled, but together, they pursued their goal of happyness [sic] and achieved it. They had a very clear *ideal* to create a better life.

When you are very clear on what your ideal is for your life, it is easier to make decisions and answer any question or opportunity that arises. If your goal is to have a well-paying career that you love, then you will consider each opportunity that comes your way based on whether it supports that goal or not. If you are considering this, first look at your current career or job. Does it help support that goal or not? Perhaps there is a skill or experience level in your current job that can serve as a stepping-stone. Alternatively, perhaps the current job provides financial means while you build toward your dream job. On the other hand, perhaps this job is the total opposite of your goal. If the job is not in support of your goal, then you need to consider a new job.

Although my near-death experience many years ago revealed my ideal was to be a healer and teacher, my banking career still served as my stepping-stone. My banker salary paid the bills, and I learned valuable skills about running a business by getting to know my banking clients' businesses. I let go of the banking stepping-stone at the appropriate time.

Aaron remembers how he applied his ideal when he was in massage school. "My ideal was to become the best healer I could be. I stated it as, 'I am Aaron, the Bringer of Light.' Even today, many years later, my ideal serves as my focus and my lighthouse beacon. If I had chosen to limit myself to an ideal of being the best massage therapist, I would not be the multidimensional healer that I am today."

If you do not know what you love to do, then you need to give yourself time to slow down and discover (or rediscover) what makes your heart sing. If you need to contemplate but friends invite you to vacation with them at a wild party-oriented resort, then stop and ask yourself this question: "Does this wild vacation support my goals, or would a calmer atmosphere better support them?" In order to gain insight into yourself and your ideals, you may need to go bicycling, go hiking, read books, write in a dream journal, try a few hobbies as experiments, and spend time with friends who are also looking to discover what they truly love to do. Alternatively, you may need time to meditate, take a leisurely bubble bath, or to do something mindless (such as ponder upon your navel or gaze off into space). If you are stressed, you may truly need to go on a spiritual retreat or attend a meditation class or get therapeutic massage on a regular basis.

How does the law of ideals interact with the law of cause and effect? Consider the following example: You start a business with the intention (ideal) of employing disadvantaged people. A number of years pass, and circumstances eventually cause you to lay off some people. If your intentions have stayed true, then the law of ideals overrides any karmic cause and effect. On the other hand, if you strayed from the original ideals and became overly greedy and self-serving, then karma will come into play. Potentially, the karmic effect is the total failure of the business.

The amazing part of the law of ideals is what the universe does to support you. Once you set a clear ideal or put a goal in place—and you truly mean it—the universe will take care of the details. Here's a funny story about this concept: My parents were going to move in with Aaron and me, but we had a shortage of storage space for their belongings. As we looked around, we found the most logical and practical solution was a new garage that would be bigger. Therefore, Aaron and I expressed the need to God for a new garage. We set forth that ideal and did what we could to support it in our daily thoughts, affirmations, and actions, including the act of buying some lottery tickets (which was unusual for us), and we patiently awaited the support of the universe to take care of this issue.

Not much later, one very cold wintry day, Aaron came inside from our workshop in the small garage where he had been making some of our healing products. He said, "Honey, not only do we no longer have a workshop, we no longer have a garage!" I was sure he was joking because that couldn't be true. He escorted me outside and showed me that our garage had totally collapsed, with one corner of the roof leaning against a small tree. Luckily, the tree withstood the weight long enough to allow us to rescue some belongings from the workshop space.

Oh, boy. At first, it was hard to see how God was *helping* us by collapsing our garage. On some level, we expected something more like winning the lottery or an enormous increase in product sales or workshop attendees to bring us the new garage. Well, fortunately, we had insurance coverage. We had partial financial support to build the garage we needed. The moral of the story is this: *Never judge the package in which your ideal arrives.* Sometimes it takes some time to recognize the fact that you have reached your goal.

One of our clients who used the techniques in the next exercise had her dream job arrive on her doorstep. The new company told Jessica that the job was hers but that she could not begin it for two months when the company began its new budget year. She was exhausted and stressed at her existing job. She was anxious to quit the job she hated and limp by until the dream job began. However, I kept getting an intuitive message for her to stay and be silent at her existing job for at least a few weeks. She reluctantly listened to me. About ten days later, she called with great excitement to announce that her current employer terminated her and gave her a twelve-week severance package. Not only was she going to have a paid vacation in the interim, but she would also have overlapping pay periods with the new job and time to do more self-healing work in between the jobs.

Think of your ideal(s) as your guiding light(s) for your life. Your actions and decisions are in alignment with and based on these principles. Once you establish your ideals consciously, your life will have vision, purpose, passion, and fulfillment. Decision-making becomes easier because if opportunities or choices are not in harmony with your ideals, it only takes an easy "No, thank you."

Exercises for the Law of Ideals

Exercise #1

Relax for a few minutes, and think of a few things that you feel or have felt very happy about: activities, hobbies, some of your positive attitudes or beliefs, certain people who are a pleasure to be around, observing a sunrise or sunset, etc. Jot down these happy things on paper, allowing for writing room between each item on the list. Try to list at least six enjoyable experiences or activities. It does not matter if they come from a period very long ago, a more recent time, or even an imagined circumstance. How does it feel to think about these experiences? What do you notice in your body and your mind? Are you more relaxed? Is it easier to breathe? Do you have a warm, comfortable feeling in your chest? Do you like this feeling? If yes, why?

If you do not have a *happy list* at the end of fifteen to twenty minutes, then write down your six most uncomfortable or unfulfilling activities, hobbies, experiences, attitudes, beliefs, etc. Examples may include impatience with my kids, an impulse to yell at my spouse, the need to be in control, or a disdain for preparing meals for the family. Leave room for writing between each item. After the list is complete, write down the *opposite* of your unpleasant experiences. For example, if you have a job where your boss is critical and negative, you might have written down, "Feel stupid and belittled at work, depressed." The opposite might be something like this: "Feel intelligent, productive, and empowered at work, ambitious." This opposite becomes your goal or ideal for that situation. As above, how does it feel to think about the positive version of what you have written?

Whichever method you chose, take your six pleasant attitudes or experiences and write down a word that captures the feeling of your goal or ideal. In fact, you may find that as you look at your list, you might have one word that captures several of them. You are choosing words that turn those positive feelings and experiences into desired *qualities* for yourself and your life relationships. Think of selecting words that are important to you, things that you would not want to go without. For the work example, perhaps "respect" or "communication" could serve as your chosen words.

Other examples of powerful word choices you may consider include love, patience, compassion, hope, honesty, commitment, trust, understanding, joy, humor, forgiveness, kindness, gentleness, faith, inner peace, or integrity.

Next, scan your list of potential ideals or guiding principles. Do any of the words capture or overlap each other? Try to narrow your list to three or fewer ideals. As you select your final words, recognize them as your lighthouse beacons to help you stay focused on your destination for your life. These ideals ultimately are about everything in your life: jobs, relationships, hobbies, where you live, what you buy, etc.

Exercise #2

Take a situation or an interpersonal relationship you would like to improve, such as the work situation in the example above. Examine this to see if your past attitudes, behaviors, and actions have been supportive of your ideals. Next, ask what steps you can take now to work toward your ideal for the situation.

In a work example, you and your boss may be triggering something unresolved deep within each other. (The boss may trigger your troubled relationship with a scolding parent when you were a child, and your boss may feel threatened by your advanced degree.) However, let us keep this part simple for now. There is a difference between your current situation and what you desire. You cannot control or change your boss. Nevertheless, you can change what *you choose* to do. Remember your free will from the law of divine oneness outlined in chapter 2.

Engage your wise and compassionate observer. Create some space between your emotions/ego and your wise observer. (See chapter 3.) Ask yourself, "What can I do?" You may get a sense of your own past triggers, but try not to name or characterize your boss's triggers or even his attitudes toward you. You might be inaccurate about the other person, but you can likely be honest with yourself.

Perhaps you will decide to request a short meeting with your boss to explain calmly that you would like to work with him to accomplish the department's goals. You can admit that you feel discouraged, and you can seek some clear guidelines on how to improve your role in the department. Ask your boss, "Can the two of us meet briefly every week so I can ask questions and get clarification? Can we e-mail priorities and action steps?"

Try to be constructive and nonjudgmental in your communication with your boss (or whomever you choose) while you stay focused on your ideal. It is important not to label *what* he has done or *why* or to put words in his mouth about how he feels about you. It is often best to make written notes in advance so that you can stay on track. Also, try to be respectful of your boss's time by being brief and to the point.

Whether your action steps involve directly speaking with your boss or simply changing your attitudes and behaviors, take time at the beginning of each day to remind yourself of your chosen ideals. Choose to take action and speak in support of what you desire as your goals. Try this every day for one month. At the end of the month, ask yourself, "What do I notice? How do I feel? What has changed? What do I need to work on more? What have I learned?"

Affirmation for the Law of Ideals

Speak this affirmation aloud slowly, deliberately and from your heart with feeling: "I am (your name). I embody trust, honesty, and patience (or your three chosen ideals) in my thoughts, words, and actions with others and myself today. The Universal Oneness (or God) supports me fully, and I accept each moment as part of the manifestation of this plan."

Repeat this at least nine times—three times each for your body, your mind, and your spirit. You may repeat this as many times throughout the day as you like. Take five to ten minutes to set a great tone for your daily activities.

We recommend that you use your affirmation with the associated Stone Play crystal layout on page 54, which will enhance your affirmation experience for the law of ideals.

This Stone Play layout creates the frequency or energy of living in accordance with ideals. Sit on a chair over it, lie on a table above it, or sit near it. Be in a quiet, receptive space to experience that frequency. Allow it to vibrate cellular memory or structure to open you up to more lightness of being.

Pay attention to subtle body sensations, images, or thoughts that come up.

You may choose to work further with your chosen ideals by applying them to your relationships with your partner, children, siblings, or parents.

Stone Play Crystal Layout
for the Law of Ideals

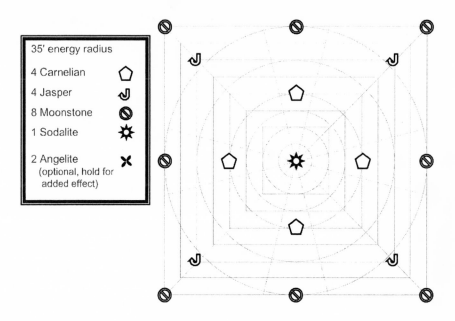

35' energy radius

4 Carnelian ⬠

4 Jasper ♪

8 Moonstone ⊘

1 Sodalite ☀

2 Angelite ✖
(optional, hold for
added effect)

© *2012 The Way to Balance, LLC*

THE LAW OF ATTRACTION (MANIFESTATION)

As [a man] thinketh in his heart, so he is.
—Jewish proverb

Artist: Alyssa Couture. © 2012 The Way to Balance, LLC

Chapter 6

The Law of Attraction (Manifestation)

This concept comes from Hinduism, Theosophy, esoteric mystery texts, Jewish proverbs, and pragmatic Christianity. More recently, it was popularized by the work of Esther and Jerry Hicks (2004, 2006) and later by the movie and book *The Secret* (Byrne, 2006).

We were grateful that the concept of universal laws gained mainstream attention since the popularization of the law of attraction (LOA). Individuals who would never have known about the existence of certain principles suddenly got excited.

As the years have passed, many students of LOA have told us they are discouraged that it has not worked for them. Worse yet, they feel like they are to blame because they are not doing LOA properly.

LOA teachers and students originally seemed to think that LOA was *the answer*, the *secret* we had all been waiting for. Yet we recognized that the truth is, LOA is only one of nine universal laws. All nine laws work together synergistically as a team. When someone only understands and works with one law instead of the complete team, many imbalances occur. Isolating one law is much like trying to build a house with only carpenters, without having an architectural blueprint or infrastructure specialists. We will cover that further in chapter 11.

Summary of the Law of Attraction

We see this law explained in these common phrases: "Like attracts like." "You are a living magnet." "Birds of a feather flock together."

Our thoughts, words, deeds, and unresolved cellular memories create an energy frequency that draws similar material things, people, and experiences into our physical lives. We *are already manifesting* in our daily lives. We are already creating our experiences *un*consciously through our *self-talk, subconscious,* or other *unresolved issues* and other actions. Often we do not like what we are creating. Negative self-talk *does* manifest for us. Whatever we talk about with ourselves or whatever deeper issues remain unresolved, we will attract those very things into our lives. In other words, we get back what we think about—whether wanted or unwanted. The law of attraction is neutral.

This law is also known as the law of manifestation, the law of vibration/energy, the law of intentional creation, and the law of intentional manifestation. The latter two names are the more developed versions of the law. This law works very powerfully and smoothly when you are clearly working from the infrastructure put in place by applying the law of ideals. Without ideals, you are likely to be subject to scattered thoughts and actions. Thus, what you manifest may not be what you truly desire.

Every invention begins with a thought or idea before it manifests itself into physical form as a new invention. Someone had a thought or inspiration as he or she observed round rocks rolling. That thought eventually led to inventing the wheel. Before a person built the first chair, someone had a thought or an idea about it. These thoughts have an energy frequency that ripples outward and attracts similar things to us. The frequency we emit also affects other people. We all know people who leave us feeling drained and unhappy after we have spent time with them. We also know people who uplift and energize us.

Someone I knew a long time ago had a pessimistic, negative attitude. Even when great opportunities came his way, his self-defeatist attitude caused him to ignore or destroy the opportunities. Even when a family member introduced him to a famous and successful person in the artistic field, where the young man showed particular gifts, he never followed through. The young man then had a series of accidents and injuries, one of which nearly killed him. This cycle went on for a number of years until he decided to pay more attention to some of the positive people and situations in his life. Although the "positives" were there all along, his energy, thoughts, and conversations with others totally amplified the "negatives" and drowned out the "positives." Once he shifted his attitude, it did not take long—only a matter of months—before his luck seemed to change for the better.

I am an example of how deeply embedded *cellular memory* can broadcast a very different message than our conscious thoughts or actions. A neighbor sexually molested me from age six to twelve, and I narrowly escaped rape during several assaults in my teens and early twenties. I was raped in my thirties. I never emotionally felt like a victim, and I was a positive, helpful person to others. I was a very successful student all the way through graduate school. My mind had made peace with those earlier incidents. Nevertheless, my body literally held those memories stuck in the cells and told the world a completely different story. It was as though I had a giant "V" for victim stamped on my forehead. I was sexually harassed at two different professional jobs following my MBA degree. I experienced more assaults. People took advantage of me financially, and I was in an abusive long-term relationship. Yet during this entire time, if you saw me walking down the street, my physical appearance and posture appeared confident and strong. I had a successful career in banking. No one even knew about the hardships and challenges I was going through. At the same time, my cellular memory was broadcasting a victim energy frequency to the world at large, and that was attracting a stream of similar situations to me.

What did I do to break this cycle? The first thing I did was to have an honest look at myself and recognize the theme in my life regarding those types of people and situations. Because I was having a number of health problems, I read *Women's Bodies, Women's Wisdom* by Christiane Northrup, MD (reprint 2010). I recognized direct connections between my life experiences that I *thought* had been healed and my physical ailments. I decided that I was ready to live my life differently. I began meditating more regularly. I started taking classes and workshops to learn self-care. I had specialized bodywork and energy work to stimulate releases from deep in the body tissue. My health problems began to melt away. Moreover, the universe really pushed that to a quantum leap. My subsequent car accident and near-death experience propelled me to become the medical intuitive and healer that I am today. I know that each and every experience, pleasant or uncomfortable, has polished me just as tumbling crystals brings out their shine and color.

What this really means is if your health and your life are everything you desire them to be, then you are already practicing part of this law. If you have anything you would pick as a higher goal or an improvement, then you have a choice to create something different and better.

Successfully working with the law of attraction also requires us to recognize that we cannot judge the package that the answer to our request comes in as Aaron and I did at first with the collapse of the garage.

There is a story about a man caught in a flood in his town. He was standing on his porch and watching the water rise when a big truck pulled up with rescuers offering to drive him to safety. He replied, "No, thanks. *God* will save me." The water continued to rise, and the streets became rivers. Shortly thereafter, some rescuers came by in a boat and invited him into the boat. He replied, "No, thanks. *God* will save me. You go ahead and help some others who need your help." The boat left, and the water rose all the way to the second floor of his home. The man climbed up on the roof. Men came by in a helicopter, but he sent them away as well when he said, "No, thanks. *God* will save me. You go ahead and help some others who need your help." Later, the rushing water swept the man off his roof, and he drowned. When he arrived in heaven, he was frustrated and disappointed (or perhaps even angry and disillusioned). He said to St. Peter, "Why did God let me drown? Why didn't he save me?" St. Peter replied, "God sent you a truck, a boat, and a helicopter. You turned down all three of God's rescues."

The man had a very clear ideal that God was going to save him, and God did try to save him. The thing is, though, we need to take action and say *yes* to the rescue. Let us not so narrowly describe our packages that we turn away the delivery people.

Our free will gives us the choice to do intentional manifestation, which is the more developed version of the law. This version works by combining techniques from the laws of unconditional love, ideals, universal abundance, and balance. We will address combining the first three in chapter 8, "The Law of Abundance."

We all have within us the power to change the conditions of our lives. Because we are already manifesting anyway, we can choose to manifest *better* things. We have the ability to transmute lower vibrations with higher vibrations. It is very important to recognize that the basic level of this law is a very powerful builder, but it is neither your architect nor the entire construction team.

Energy or Vibration

As we discussed in chapter 2, "The Law of Divine Oneness," all matter is comprised of energy in motion. As humans, our understanding that matter exists is based on our ability to touch, smell, see, hear, or taste it. Our senses tell us that a rock is solid, but an electron microscope shows us that a rock is truly composed of vibrating atoms whose protons, electrons, and neutrons are in constant movement. The frequency at which atoms vibrate determines whether H_2O is ice, water, or steam.

The difference between the physical, mental, and spiritual aspects of our human selves and those same dimensions in the universe is the vibration rate of the atoms/energy. We all know that, we as humans cease to hear beyond a certain sound frequency rate, yet dogs and other animals still hear. We also know that the visible light spectrum (colors we can see) is very small in comparison to the full electromagnetic spectrum. Average human senses cannot see X-rays, cosmic rays, long-wave rays, etc. Yet they exist.

The same principle applies to our thoughts and words. They are energy too. Positive, uplifting, powerful thoughts and words vibrate faster than negative ones. Negative, limiting thoughts create resistance, an actual contraction within you. Notice how your body feels heavy and tense when you think negative thoughts. Fortunately, the higher vibrations win as long as your focus goes there.

If you tone a C-note musical tuning fork next to a second C-note tuning fork, the second one will also vibrate. Objects and thoughts tend to vibrate faster in the presence of higher vibrating objects and thoughts. For example, have you ever noticed how a high-energy, positive person helps everyone around him or her feel better? This is energy resonance. You can apply this concept to raise your energy vibration. You attract more of what you give out, so it is important to practice projecting the type of energy you would like to receive.

Think of your thoughts as investments. *Do I want more of this investment? Do I like the nest egg in which I have invested? If not, what investment do I want to make instead?* Being human means having a steady stream of thoughts flow through your mind. The more you focus your thought stream on positive investments, the more you attract and build the investment you desire.

This can be particularly challenging when we find ourselves in a very difficult predicament, or so our human ego tells us. As an example, take a person who experiences financial devastation, losing his job and home. On first inclination, one may want to say, "How horrible," or blame the boss or company who let him go for causing this mess. It is only when we create a conflict with *what is* that we would judge this as *horrible*. With the flow and exchange in the universe, we cannot say it *should not* have happened, because it *did happen*. The moment we *accept* that it happened, we are free of the conflict, inner resistance, and struggle. The lower vibrations are released, and we are free to build a new investment.

In *Tao Te Ching*, Lao-tzu tells a story of highly respected Zen Master Hakuin in Japan. Many people venerated him and came to learn his spiritual wisdom. Then one day, his neighbor's teenage daughter became pregnant. Her angry parents questioned her repeatedly, "Who is the father?" She finally answered that it was Zen Master Hakuin. Her outraged parents ran to Master Hakuin, yelling and accusing him, saying their daughter had confessed that he was the father. Master Hakuin simply replied, "Is that so?"

The scandalous news spread quickly and destroyed the master's reputation. This did not trouble him. When the baby was born, the parents delivered him to Hakuin. "You are the father, so you look after him." Hakuin lovingly cared for the baby. After about a year, the child's mother confessed to her parents that Master Hakuin was not the father. It was a young man in town. Her parents were very upset and went to apologize and beg forgiveness of the master. "We are really sorry. We have come to take the baby back. Our daughter confessed that you are not the father."

The master replied, "Is that so?" as he turned the child over to them (Lao-tzu, translation 1988).

Master Hakuin did not judge or label the words or events. Whether it was the truth or a lie, good or bad news, his reply is unchanged: "Is that so?" He was totally in the moment as a witness. His *acceptance of what was* caused no inner resistance or struggle. He stayed in the higher vibrations. The law of divine oneness permeates everything—everything is good.

The law of attraction/manifestation also requires applying the law of polarity, the masculine and the feminine energy principles, which we address in the following chapter.

Exercise for the Law of Attraction

Write down the three ideals you chose from the prior chapter. Next, select a concrete goal you would like to achieve. For example, you may have honesty, compassion, and joy as your ideals. Your concrete goal may be to own a car or a home.

Either type on a computer or clip from magazines the words "honesty," "compassion," "joy," "home," "car," (or your selected ideals and concrete goals) in a bold, attractive font. Also, clip or scan photos that give you the feelings of those words. Use photos similar to the car or home you desire. It is helpful to pick a realistic goal based on your current situation as you will manifest those results quicker.

Paste these onto a poster board, tack them to a bulletin board, or create your beautiful collage in electronic form on the computer. This is your vision board or goal board. Place it somewhere close to you so that you look at it multiple times each day. Daydream or meditate with it. Feel, visualize, or imagine what it feels like in your body and in your heart to have achieved this concrete goal, which is in alignment with your ideals.

If your concrete goal is a certain amount of money in your bank account, you may decide to photocopy a current bank account statement and add several zeros to the deposit figures and then retotal your balances. Alternatively, take a one-dollar bill and add many zeros to it and keep it in your wallet or paste it to your goal-board collage.

It is important to work simultaneously with your ideals as you work on your goal(s). For example, if your concrete goal is to have a certain amount of money in your bank account, your ideal of "honesty" or "integrity" sets in motion your standards and principles for obtaining the money. If you choose ruthless or dishonest means to reach your concrete goal, the law of cause and effect (karma) will activate.

Spend time daily with your vision board for at least forty-five days. Meditate on it, visualize it, and feel it in your heart. Make your daily decisions based on being in alignment with the ideals and concrete goals on the board. Although you may spend more time on it each day, ten to fifteen minutes daily is very powerful. See what you manifest.

Once you have accomplished a few easier goals, your confidence and trust in the process will empower you to build higher and higher goals. You may decide to create more vision boards over time.

Keep in mind that sometimes it takes the universe time to manifest fully the concrete goal, but know that the universe is manifesting for you. The more you can support that with positive thoughts, words, and actions, the easier it is.

Affirmation for the Law of Attraction

As you personalize this affirmation, we suggest you choose a very clear and simply stated manifestation desire. For example, if you desire a love relationship, "my ideal life partner" is perfectly stated. If you start describing conditions and details, you are limiting your universe. If you describe a religious requirement, income levels, race, height, eye color, etc., you are attempting to control the package.

Speak this affirmation aloud slowly and deliberately from your heart with feeling: "I co-create with God/Spirit to manifest my heart's deepest desires. The love in my heart draws *my ideal life partner* directly to me. I am grateful for *my ideal life partner.*"

Other examples may include inner peace, joy, ideal career, a true friend, my next mentor, etc. "I co-create with God/Spirit to manifest my heart's deepest desires. The love in my heart draws _____ (your desired manifestation) directly to me. I am grateful for _____."

Repeat this at least nine times—three times each for your body, your mind, and your spirit. You may repeat this as many times throughout the day as you like. Take five to ten minutes to set a great tone for your daily activities.

We recommend that you use your affirmation with the associated Stone Play crystal layout on the following page, which will enhance your affirmation experience for the law of attraction.

This Stone Play layout creates the frequency or energy of empowering attraction/manifestation. Sit on a chair over it, lie on a table above it, or sit near it. Be in a quiet, receptive space to experience that frequency. Allow it to vibrate cellular memory or structure to open you up to more lightness of being.

Pay attention to subtle body sensations, images, or thoughts that come up.

Stone Play Crystal Layout
for the Law of Attraction/Manifestation

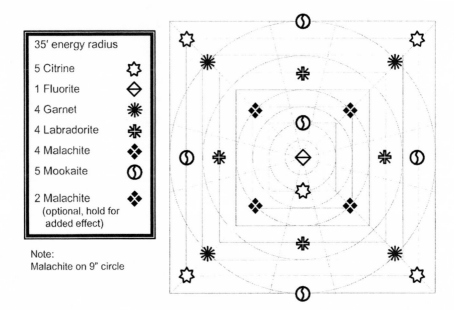

35' energy radius	
5 Citrine	✡
1 Fluorite	⬙
4 Garnet	✳
4 Labradorite	✴
4 Malachite	❖
5 Mookaite	☽
2 Malachite (optional, hold for added effect)	❖

Note:
Malachite on 9" circle

© 2012 The Way to Balance, LLC

THE LAW
OF POLARITY

Logic must be tempered by the wisdom of our hearts.
—The Essenes

Artist: Alyssa Couture. © 2012 The Way to Balance, LLC

Chapter 7

The Law of Polarity (Balance)

This is also called the law of harmony, the law of balance, and the law of gender. Everything has its masculine (yang) and feminine (yin) aspects. All creation is based on balance or harmony between the two. In order for someone to master co-creating with God, this harmony between male and female must exist within.

The masculine (yang) energy is expansion, action, and electrical in nature. The female (yin) energy is drawing inward, attraction, intuitive, and magnetic in nature. Together, these two form our electromagnetic balance. This electromagnetic aspect is visible as our energy field or aura, and it can be viewed through Kirlian photography and other specialty devices. Some of us can see or perceive it naturally without the use of equipment. All of us can develop this capacity to see auras naturally with practice and intention. Christian, Buddhist, and Hindu art from long ago represented the aura as the halos around spiritually active people. Although all of us have auras, the aura is usually more intense, stronger, and more visible in people who incorporate spiritual or energy practices in their daily lives, such as those who live in harmony with the law of polarity.

For many aspects in our lives, certain cycles restore balance or harmony. In the course of a twenty-four-hour day, your two nostrils and sides of your sinuses take turns being the primary intake. Your liver, kidneys, and other organs and glands have different cycles during which they each cleanse and restore. It is impossible for all your systems in your body to cleanse and restore themselves at the same time. The detoxification process is a very different activity than the rebuilding process, and both require many of your body's energy resources. Moreover, both seemingly opposite cycles are necessary to maintain life.

Male (sperm) and female (egg) create life by joining together. The synergistic response between them is conception, which starts a new life. Whether we are male or female, we all have both masculine and feminine energy aspects. Our inner knowing, intuition, sacred hearts, the right hemispheres of our brains, autonomic nervous system, emotions, and gut instincts are all feminine. Our actions, intellect, analytical logic, the left hemisphere of our brains, sympathetic nervous system, and conscious minds are all masculine. Although we all possess and utilize both aspects, most people tend to favor one over the other. However, the law of polarity requires that we are equally adept with left and right brain activity. Once we are comfortable with both *intellect* (masculine) and *intuition* (feminine), we can become powerful co-creators with God.

A recent review of US presidents and presidential candidates provides an interesting analogy. As of 2012, five of the last seven (71.4 percent) US presidents were either left-handed or ambidextrous (Chung, 2008, Rotstein, 2008). Because left-handedness used to be considered a disability and teachers attempted to switch students to right-handedness into the 1950s and 1960s, it is difficult to determine the natural handedness with absolute certainty before then. In the overall population, approximately 10 to 12 percent are ambidextrous or left-handed, yet approximately 50 percent of the US presidents since 1929 are that "minority." Naturally, the right hemisphere of the brain controls the left side of the body. It appears that left-handed people tend to process language and complex reasoning via both sides of the brain. Does this mean lefties are more intelligent or capable? No, not necessarily. In fact, many lefties are actually ambidextrous, forced by being in the minority.

When I was a child, we did not have any left-handed scissors in our home. When I was in elementary school, two of us in my class were lefties, yet each classroom had only one set of left-handed scissors. I got tired of waiting for the other lefty to finish each project, so I started cutting with my right hand. The teacher always demonstrated writing, and she did everything with her right hand. I tried it both ways. Initially, I drew, painted, and wrote interchangeably with either hand. I learned how to play sports and play the guitar with my right hand. I rode my horse western-style, so that was left-handed reining. To this day, my stronger arm is my right. I prefer writing with my left, and I paint walls and woodwork with either hand. At a crowded table, I will eat with the hand that has more elbow room from my neighbor.

When one uses both sides of the body for various ambidextrous activities, he or she also stimulates both sides of the brain, and consequently, they work together very effectively. Taking this observation another step further, both hemispheres working to *co-create* means that someone can easily adapt, and these people tend to gather a combination of analytical/logical (masculine) data and intuitive/sensing (feminine) inner knowing. This capacity to adapt and use both sides of the brain may be a very important quality for leadership abilities, such as being a president.

Living according to the law of polarity applies both masculine and feminine aspects. A battery provides a good illustration. A battery has a positive end (masculine) and a negative end (feminine). When either of the two ends loses its contact point, you have no power. As soon as the circuit is completed with the feminine and masculine parts connected, power is restored. The opposites need to interact to create energy and movement. The battery will not work without both the male and female ends working together.

Intuition and manifestation require both yin (feminine) and yang (masculine) energy working in combination with each other. Going back to the battery example, the masculine sends energy out (+ pole of the battery) and the feminine energy receives (– pole of the battery). Telepathy between two people means one person sends the thought or performs an action (masculine energy) and another person receives the thought or perceives the action (feminine energy).

This may explain why so many people who are constant doers or givers may become psychically blocked. They rarely give themselves permission to slow down and to receive. This is very common in individuals who work in high-stress and extremely competitive jobs. The energy of the job is overly masculine. As a balance, we recommend to our students that they follow the steps and actions of the protocols we recommend. The protocols provide masculine action. Then we suggest they simply relax, allow, and make sure they are willing to receive (feminine drawing in).

In other words, when you try too hard to make an intuitive insight happen, you are making too big of an effort, and your male energy is blocking it from happening. Receptivity is the female energy required in order to receive intuitive insights. It is also possible to be overly feminine in energy actions. You can become a passive person who watches instead of doing activities. Learning to both give and receive is healthy. This balance is required in order to activate fully the law of manifestation.

The yin/yang balance does not necessarily mean that the feminine and masculine aspects are in equal amounts. Each individual is slightly more masculine or feminine in nature. This balance is about allowing both to be present, recognizing them, and utilizing the gifts both energies have to offer.

An excellent example is something that happened with my brother, Jason, when we lived on the farm. We required a lot of firewood to heat our home, and used a hydraulic log splitter to split the firewood. The logs would come out of the splitter and pile up in a disorganized manner. We then had to manually pick up the logs and load them into a truck. It was time-consuming and labor-intensive to stop the splitter every few minutes and transfer the split logs onto the truck. Jason adapted a hay-bale conveyor belt to do the job, but the belt kept shutting down when he was splitting. He wracked his brain trying to solve the problem. He eventually realized that the hydraulic power used by the splitter was robbing the power for the conveyor. They would not run simultaneously, and switching the power back and forth between the splitter and conveyor did not help because the logs would not automatically flow as intended. Jason used his intellect and analytical brain to try to figure it out. He tried several things, and none of them worked. This was masculine energy activity. Finally, he got frustrated and gave up. He kept stopping the splitter and moved the pile of split logs by hand the usual way.

Within a day or two when he awoke in the morning, Jason remembered a dream wherein he had solved the problem. He sat and reflected on the dream to remember the details. This was feminine energy activity. He went out to the barn and did precisely what was in the dream. He created a T-splitter for the hydraulic line, fed in a second source of hydraulic power, and thus allowed both log splitter and conveyor belt to run efficiently. It worked! The problem was solved, and farm life became easier.

In our dream state, we are open to our intuition. We are able to find solutions that our intellectual minds do not yet know. Connecting with God and manifesting from that divine inspiration involves both the masculine and the feminine aspects within us. The prayer, request, or activity is the masculine energy. The dream state, meditation, or receiving is the feminine energy. Electricity is created by the flow between both the positive pole and the negative pole of the battery. Conception is the result of male and female joining.

Exercise for the Law of Polarity

Take a ruler and balance it horizontally on your index finger. Everyone obviously knows where to place his or her finger to balance the ruler so that it is equally weighted on each end.

Now place a quarter on one end of the ruler and a dime on the other. Attempt to intuitively rest or balance the ruler on your index finger at the optimal location. Adjust it until you succeed in balancing the ruler.

Imagine that the quarter represents the mode you spend the most time in. Is it analytical, logical thinking or performing tasks or duties? On the other hand, is it creative, expressive, meditative, and intuitive? What are some steps you can take to bring more of the lighter-weighted side (the one you use less than the other) into your life?

If you lean heavily on the analytical/thinking mode, some ways you can explore your other side might include the following:

- Start a dream journal.
- Practice meditation.
- Practice Chi Kung.
- Listen to music.
- Paint.
- Practice Tai Chi.
- Practice yoga.
- Garden in a gentle, relaxed manner.

- Partake in photography, artwork, or craft hobbies.
- Write poetry.
- Spend time in nature.
- Read inspirational books.

If you lean heavily on the intuitive/meditative mode, some ways you can explore your other side might include the following:

- Swim.
- Run.
- Play tennis.
- Play squash.
- Go horseback riding.
- Read a more technical article or book about a subject you find interesting, but perhaps one that is not your typical choice.
- Take a class that is more technical than your typical choice.
- Complete a project you started but have not yet completed.
- Write down a set of instructions or how-to steps for a household or work task as though you are teaching someone else how to perform the task.
- Volunteer to help a friend or a charitable organization with activities like delivery, packaging, cleaning, and cooking.

Some people may think that being in the meditative mode all the time is a good thing, but think again. If you have a brilliant idea or invention, but you never actually build it or follow through on it, you never completely manifest it. If One Source lets you know that you are a healer, your logic will hopefully kick in to prevent you from resigning from your job the next day. Instead, you would allow the details about paying your living expenses work themselves out with paychecks.

I was a banker, and my near-death experience from a car accident revealed that my life's purpose was to be a healer and a teacher. Yet it took eight years of transition until I could resign from my job. In fact, I was surprised when my intuition gave me a clear message that I needed to change jobs and work at another bank (rather than become a full-time healer and teacher). I was already working very long hours in the banking field, and I was also working very long hours in the evenings and on the weekends in the healing and teaching field.

How did I have time to look for another banking job? Because my life purpose was to become a healer and teacher, why would I seek another position in banking? My message from God assured me that I had more to accomplish in the business world and that the details of manifesting the job were already in process. However, I needed to put together my resume. That resume was my *masculine energy* action step, my analytical, logical task. I felt driven and compelled to update my resume immediately.

I had just handed my resume to a friend for his critique and feedback when I received a phone call unexpectedly from a headhunter. He precisely described me and my dream job in the banking field. In order to interview me, they required a resume first. Yes, I got the job, and it was a wonderful opportunity and experience. It was a true win-win for both my employer and me. I accomplished a five-year business plan for them in under one year, and several members of management acknowledged that I had somehow touched their hearts and changed how they viewed the world. Now it was evident to me *why* I was supposed to go to another banking position first before I expanded my healing and teaching lifework to full-time.

If spirit tells you that your ideal partner will arrive in your life, you cannot sit at home alone and wait for the mail and the telephone. You must participate. You must be out living, acting, and following through in order to find each other. A few decades ago, I began to reflect on my ideal life partner by applying the law of ideals and putting those ideal traits in writing. I actively dated, attended workshops, played tennis, and traveled with friends or on my own to destinations that appealed to me. A few years later, I learned about a one-week meditation class that I wanted to take in Virginia Beach. None of my friends was available to go, so I went ahead and booked a solo trip. I went because I really wanted to go. Lo and behold, that was where I met Aaron. If I had stayed at home because I was afraid to travel alone or because I thought *Mr. Right* would simply knock on my door, I would have missed meeting my most amazing and wonderful husband.

Therefore, the moral of the story is to remember to engage both your yin and your yang to manifest your dreams.

Affirmation for the Law of Polarity

Speak this affirmation aloud slowly and deliberately from your heart with feeling: "I embody balance as I cycle though the natural phases of activity and quiet contemplation. The ebb and flow of the ocean tides restore harmony for the planet and me automatically and wherever I am."

Repeat this at least nine times—three times each for your body, your mind, and your spirit. You may repeat this as many times throughout the day as you like. Take five to ten minutes to set a great tone for your daily activities.

We recommend that you use your affirmation with the associated Stone Play crystal layout on the following page, which will enhance your affirmation experience for the law of polarity.

This Stone Play layout creates the frequency or energy of balance/polarity. Sit on a chair over it, lie on a table above it, or sit near it. Be in a quiet, receptive space to experience that frequency. Allow it to vibrate cellular memory or structure to open you up to more lightness of being.

Pay attention to subtle body sensations, images, or thoughts that come up.

Stone Play Crystal Layout
for the Law of Polarity/Balance

25' energy radius

1 Blue Lace
  Agate   ⌘

4 Carnelian   ⬠

4 Rose Quartz   ✴

4 Selenite   ▱

2 Lapis Lazuli   ⚔
  (optional, hold for
  added effect)

Note:
Selenite on 18" circle
Rose Quartz on 24" circle

© 2012 The Way to Balance, LLC

THE LAW OF ABUNDANCE

People with a scarcity mentality tend to see everything in terms of win-lose. There is only so much; and if someone else has it, that means there will be less for me. The more principle-centered we become, the more we develop an abundance mentality, the more we are genuinely happy for the successes, well-being, achievements, recognition, and good fortune of other people. We believe their success adds to . . . rather than detracts from . . . our lives."
—Stephen R. Covey

The abundant life does not come to those who have had a lot of obstacles removed from their path by others. It develops from within and is rooted in strong mental and moral fiber.
—William Mather Lewis

When you focus on being a blessing, God makes sure that you are always blessed in abundance.
—Joel Osteen

Not what we have, but what we enjoy, constitutes our abundance.
—John Petit-Senn

To live a pure unselfish life, one must count nothing as one's own in the midst of abundance.
—Buddha

You pray in your distress and in your need; would that you might also pray in the fullness of your joy and in your days of abundance.
—Kahlil Gibran

Whatever we are waiting for—peace of mind, contentment, grace, the inner awareness of abundance—it will surely come to us, but only when we are ready to receive it with an open and grateful heart.
—Sarah Ban Breathnach

Artist: Alyssa Couture. © 2012 The Way to Balance, LLC

Chapter 8

The Law of Abundance

There is no better way to begin a chapter on abundance than with a cornucopia of quotes that show there are many aspects to abundance. As we share various quotes from differing perspectives, we begin to define it. The law of abundance is based on the true definition of the word itself: a greater plentiful amount, a profusion, fullness to overflowing, an overflowing quantity, affluence, wealth (*Webster's Encyclopedic Unabridged Dictionary*, 2001). Abundance comes from the Latin verb *abundare*, which means "to abound, to overflow." It is an energy, a feeling to tap in to or *tune in* to; overflowing abundance is an aspect of unconditional love. When Jesus and the apostles multiplied the fish and loaves of bread to feed the crowds, they applied the law of unconditional love and the law of abundance. The principles of the law of abundance are all about energy exchange and energy movement.

As Albert Einstein said, "Energy is neither created nor destroyed. It simply changes form." There is always an abundance of energy. Motion creates energy. Inside the molecules that make up every form of matter, electrons spin in orbits around the nucleus, which creates an energy exchange. Recall the exercise in chapter 2 regarding the law of divine oneness, wherein you visualized being part of a big grid of lines of light in and around the earth, a net similar to lines of latitude and longitude. Now, as an analogy, imagine this is the power grid for the networks of all the power plants providing electricity to towns and customers. Imagine each customer (you, me, every relative, every friend, etc.) as a speck of light on the grid connected by all the power lines. Each of us has a control panel to communicate when we have extra to share and tell each other what we are looking for. This process is a bit like a power and energy barter system. This is such an efficient barter system that we just post the data, and without personally knowing the individuals, the energy resources move around. Our deeper selves, our subconscious and conscious thoughts, and our beliefs are already participating in this network, fueled by the One Source, God.

You can imagine this exchange like the World Wide Web, the Internet. Craigslist, eBay, and a myriad of other sites provide networks of data—who has what to sell, barter, or trade and who is looking to purchase.

God provides a boundless flow of love and resources. It is *not* metered out. It is not "robbing Peter to pay Paul." We all have an abundance of whatever we focus the most time and energy on. Money is energy. Love is energy. Providing a service or product is energy. Moreover, life is all about exchange and the movement of energy.

As a member of a barter system (yes, you are), you must understand that you *offer* something and you *receive* something. The law of abundance requires both giving and receiving. Abundance is not given freely. It is acquired. You must exercise in order to win a triathlon. You must speak for others to hear you. You must practice to earn your driver's license. You must play the game in order to score. You must learn the material in order to receive an A+. This involves the feminine (receiving) and masculine (doing/giving) energy aspects, which we covered in chapter 7, "The Law of Polarity (Balance)."

This law requires truly knowing what is important to us in terms of our belief systems, our *self-talk* subconscious, and our verbalized consciousness. Years ago, a married couple I knew was extremely budget-oriented and tended to nickel-and-dime everything, even with each other. Alex and Nicole both got their wallets out to separately pay for fruit smoothies or museum entrance fees. For example, if the husband decided to *treat* his spouse, he would publicly announce the treat and the fact that he expected to receive the next round (which he calculated within a dollar or so between them). What a perfect example of what the law of universal abundance is *not!* They clearly held a belief system of scarcity as well as a very calculated exchange of karma. This naturally permeated their marriage as well as their friendships with others.

If you asked Alex and Nicole what was important to them, they would not have described it in the same way I have. They probably would have described it as fair and equitable calculations or something to that effect. Yet their actions demonstrated what is truly important to them: scarcity, precisely calculated karmic exchange, conditional love, and living with an agenda. When I knew them, I could see that it was already a source of stress in their young marriage, even though their beliefs were similar.

I applied the laws of unconditional love, abundance, ideals, and attraction when I was about thirteen or fourteen years old and living on a farm. We raised grapes and Christmas trees and made maple syrup to sell. My parents also both worked full-time outside the farm to make ends meet. (Note the belief system statement here.) My French teacher in the local school announced he was leading a trip to France in two years and suggested we students all start preparing to go. I was so excited and exhilarated. I was going to practice my French with real French people and visit a *foreign* land! I wondered what their clothes would be like, what the soil, plants, and trees would look like, what kind of food they eat. You would think I was about to go to Mars because the concept about what *they* were like seemed that alien to me, yet in a very positive and curious way. I loved speaking French. I was daydreaming and visualizing these upcoming adventures from the first moment the teacher announced the trip.

I excitedly announced to my parents, "I am going to France in two years on the French teacher's trip!"

My mother was totally surprised and said, "What on earth are you talking about? That trip must be very expensive, and you know we don't have enough money to send you on that trip. No, you are not going to France."

So far, my father was silent. I very quickly replied to my mother, "I didn't ask you for any money. I am going to pay for it myself."

My father then asked me *how* I was going to raise the money. "Babysitting, odd jobs for neighbors and family, etc."

At that point, my father said, "Good. I have another idea that you might try too. Those old blueberry bushes behind the barn look like they could use some attention. If you fertilize them and take care of them, you can pick and then sell the blueberries and keep all the money you make."

He took me down to look more carefully at the blueberry bushes and gave me instructions on their care. He also warned me I would not be able to sleep in during the summer when I was busy harvesting the berries. I had to pick them early and sell when fresh. I fertilized, pruned, cleaned up the rows, and proudly watched the appearance of blossoms that would lead to berries. Once the berries formed, I bought and applied special netting to protect them from the birds. Once I got started, both my mother and father encouraged me. The first year, I picked them all myself. I sold some directly to the public but sold most of them to well-visited farm stands and local grocers. The second year, I had such a bountiful harvest that I had to hire several neighbors to help me pick the berries. I counted my earnings, net of my expenses, and added in the money from my babysitting and the odd jobs I did. I had earned the money I needed to go to France. My parents ended up providing me with some spending money, as my total covered only the trip itself, without any extra to spend. My first trip to France was everything I dreamed of and more.

Exercise for the Law of Abundance

Abundance does require action. You cannot sit at home unemployed and expect abundance without taking steps to earn money. You must apply for a job or explore other avenues to create cash flow. Your thoughts, beliefs, attitudes, and actions will work together to stimulate the support of the universe.

Are your actions consistent with your beliefs about abundance? How many times in the last month have you said, "I cannot afford that," or, "I don't have any money for that"?

Take a few minutes to write down some things you frequently say related to money, scarcity, and abundance. Some examples that attract scarcity include the following: "I cannot afford that." "I wish I had enough money to go on a vacation (buy a new car, etc.)." "There is never enough money to do what I want." "I will never get out of debt." If they are concerned with anything less than pure abundance and positivity, then rewrite your phrases so that they are purely about abundance. Some statements to support abundance include the following: "I attract money continuously." "I live an abundant life." "I have an abundance of blessings and friends." "The universe provides me with abundant support."

Create your own written statements from them or use the affirmation at the end of this chapter. Either post your affirmation in places you will read it repeatedly or devise an action or exercise that symbolizes it.

A woman we know recently realized that she was defining her life in terms of scarcity. "I don't have any money" was a very common phrase for Caroline since her divorce. Someone suggested she tape money around her apartment: in the kitchen, bathroom, and bedroom. Caroline taped fifty-dollar bills in those places. Now she looks around every day and says, "Look at this! I have money everywhere!" She started talking about traveling to other countries again.

Then Caroline commented to Jennifer about her delay in completing a project for Jennifer. Caroline commented, "I'll get to it, but right now, I am looking for ways to increase my abundant cash flow."

Perhaps surprised that it was not clear before, Jennifer replied, "That project will result in income for both you and me. You will be paid a commission for the sales it creates." Was it a coincidence that this happened within a few short weeks of her taping money around her apartment and saying, "I have money everywhere," with a chuckle and a smile? Opportunity just knocked. Now Caroline needs to take the action steps to manifest the money.

Affirmation for the Law of Abundance

Speak this affirmation aloud slowly and deliberately from your heart with feeling: "My heart is abundantly flowing with capacity to give as well as receive. I live and act in prosperous ways."

Repeat this at least nine times—three times each for your body, your mind, and your spirit. You may repeat this as many times throughout the day as you like. Take five to ten minutes to set a great tone for your daily activities.

We recommend that you use your affirmation with the associated Stone Play crystal layout on page 87, which will enhance your affirmation experience for the law of abundance.

This Stone Play layout creates the frequency or energy of abundance. Sit on a chair over it, lie on a table above it, or sit near it. Be in a quiet, receptive space to experience that frequency. Allow it to vibrate cellular memory or structure to open you up to more lightness of being.

Pay attention to subtle body sensations, images, or thoughts that come up.

Stone Play Crystal Layout for the Law of Abundance

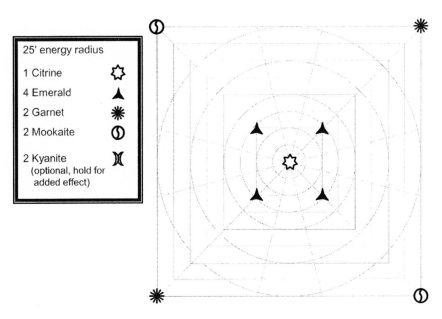

25' energy radius

1 Citrine ☆

4 Emerald ▲

2 Garnet ✳

2 Mookaite ☽

2 Kyanite)(
(optional, hold for
added effect)

© 2012 The Way to Balance, LLC

THE LAW
OF GRATITUDE

It is your resistance to "what is" that causes your suffering.
—Buddha

Artist: Alyssa Couture. © 2012 The Way to Balance, LLC

Chapter 9

The Law of Gratitude

Gratitude is a sense of appreciation, acknowledgment, thankfulness, honor, and praise for anything at all. Gratitude for both what you like and do not like completes the knowingness. How can you know what *is* without knowing what is *not*? This refers back to chapter 2, "The Law of Divine Oneness" (completing the cycle of *total knowingness*), as well as chapter 7, "The Law of Polarity (Balance)." A pendulum swings back and forth from one extreme to another. Swings of the pendulum—what you like and what you hate—are the two ends of the same thing, namely the pendulum's path. If you love spending time with your life partner and hate being separate, you are experiencing two extremes of the same essence, specifically your relationship with your partner. You are defining different aspects or defining the parameters of the relationship. It is because of the moments of absence that you appreciate the togetherness. When you become grateful for both what you like and dislike, your knowingness is complete. The completion of knowingness creates a big shift and releases the need for what you do not like!

As an example, consider Rick and Cindy, a couple who both worked long hours, and not always on the same schedule. Rick was not making as much money as he desired. Because they both loved to travel and wanted to travel more, they needed additional financial flexibility. Seemingly out of nowhere (but now you know there is no such thing as that), people he had known several years back offered Rick a consulting position, teaching companies a particular business model. He accepted this lucrative position and underwent training. His first consulting position was in London, all expenses paid, of course. He worked several weeks straight and then had ten days off. Sometimes he stayed in London and the nearby countryside to sightsee, and sometimes he came home. He had not yet built up enough frequent-flier miles to travel back and forth constantly, and he found the jetlag and adjustment quite tiring. He used some of his air miles to purchase Cindy tickets to fly to London when she could get the time off from her job. Cindy was miserably unhappy back home, depressed until each time they were together. Then her mood soared.

We asked her how their time together was going. Cindy said she was happy only when they were together. In addition, by the time a few days passed, she already began to dread their next separation. I suggested that she name several positive aspects to the entire situation, including the separation, for which she could be grateful. I spoke with her about gratitude. I reminded her that they both enjoyed the extra money and that he was learning new concepts and techniques that they might later apply to their own joint projects. Cindy also recognized that she had become quite dependent on Rick for her happiness. She could look at the separation time as a gift—a time for her to meditate and discover the peace and love within herself apart from him. The extra income allowed them to purchase some things they had previously delayed buying. By the end of our session, Cindy had several gratitude items on her list, and she already felt better.

When we saw Cindy several months later, we asked how she was doing. Her eyes lit up, and she said, "*Much* better. Our time together is sweeter and more loving than it used to be, even though we already had a great time together. I have more time for yoga and meditation when he is away. My body feels more flexible, and I have fewer aches and pains. I feel more peaceful and relaxed. I feel as though we are each creating a part of the big picture of our future together. I don't dread our separation times anymore."

Cindy successfully practiced the law of gratitude and found love and appreciation for the extremes (the together time and the separation time) and completed her *knowingness*. A few months later, she told me that Rick had put in so many work hours that he would be home most of the summer. The *need* for what she did not like is starting to go away because she no longer hates it.

Another couple was struggling financially as Sheila stayed home with their three young kids and Bob worked many hours at a job he did not like. They both wanted to return home to the Midwest, where they were born and raised, to be with family and friends.

The only apartment Bob and Sheila could afford on his income was located in a very run-down neighborhood in a city with a high crime rate. As she looked out the windows, she saw several burned out and severely damaged brick buildings. Sheila was scared and angry. She kept herself and the children inside much of the time, lamenting how much she hated it here and how much she wanted to go home to her family. Sheila kept saying, "This is not the home I want." Yet for all the time she spent inside it, she had done nothing to decorate or create a feeling of "home."

We strongly encouraged Sheila to "bloom where she was planted," to be grateful for a roof and walls, beds for all of them, the money to pay rent and to buy food. She argued at first that there was nothing beautiful about it and nothing for which she could be grateful. We challenged her to take action, to do something to enhance the beauty, to take some steps to make her house feel like home. Sheila went to some yard sales and secondhand stores in other towns, found bargain-priced beautiful posters, attractive framed pictures, window boxes, etc.

Together, Sheila and her children planted the window boxes with flowers, covered one particularly rough window view with a beautiful poster, and hung some artwork and family pictures, and she even picked up the clutter. The transformations in the little apartment—and in her—were astounding. Once Bob, Sheila, and their children found beauty and hominess in their temporary apartment, they were much happier. Some months later, Sheila announced that Bob accepted a "dream job" offer back home in the Midwest. The pay increase was substantial, and the new employer was paying all their moving expenses. Look what a bit of gratitude and "blooming where you are planted" can do for your life.

We saw an interview with a woman who had no legs from early childhood onward. The small stumps below her hips caused pain and presented her with challenges in maintaining her balance when she used her prosthetic legs, so she chose a skateboard to get around instead. She would swing herself up onto the counter to make meals. She could drive a car with special controls. She had a full-time job she loved. She shopped and cleaned house, and so on. She and her (able-bodied) husband conceived and delivered a healthy child the regular old-fashioned way. Her husband fell in love with her because he had never met such an amazing person in his entire life. It was practically love at first sight. They had spoken with each other on the phone for some time in their roles as car-parts vendor and mechanic. They learned they had a lot in common and truly enjoyed talking to each other. It never came up in conversation that she no longer had her legs. A situation arose when they needed to exchange a necessary auto part in person rather than by mail or a courier service. Therefore, they met, and he asked her out on a date, which he had been planning to do anyway. He never felt one ounce of pity for her, and in fact, she would not have liked him if he had.

We remember a question from the interviewer about how she and her parents managed to instill such a positive outlook in her despite her disability. She had a puzzled look on her face and said something to this effect: "My parents always taught me that the definition of a disabled person is someone who is not able to do everything. I *can* and *do* indeed *do everything I want to do* in life. Nothing has ever held me back. I am not disabled." She smiled a big happy smile.

Exercises for the Law of Gratitude

Exercise #1

Take a section of an orange, mango, or a fruit you love. Study it, smell it, and take in its color and texture. Reflect on how grateful you are that it has come to you, originating from a seed. Put a taste of this fruit on your tongue.

Now send all your thankfulness and gratitude into this fruit. Allow gratitude to flow from your heart down your arms through your hands and fingers into the fruit. Let your eyes radiate gratitude into the fruit. Now eat it. Does it taste better? Does it taste like the *best* fruit you have ever had in your life?

Exercise #2

Select a situation or relationship that you would like to change from what it currently is. You may choose a job/career, a romantic relationship, a friendship, a relationship with a family member, a financial or legal situation, a challenging illness/disease, or whatever else comes to the forefront for you.

If there are some aspects of this situation, relationship, etc. that you like and already feel good about, then write them down in a list. If you do not immediately think of an aspect you like, then proceed to the next step.

Write down a list of aspects you dislike or things you wish were different about the situation. Leave room off to the right-hand side for notes. Take a few minutes to reflect on something good or positive, something to be grateful for in regard to the *dislike* list. In fact, for each *negative* aspect you choose, write down at least three benefits or *positives* next to it. They can be anything, including helping you learn to rest and practice self-care, enjoying quiet and solitude, figuring out what you truly enjoy doing, having compassion for others in similar circumstances, stepping into your power and saying, "No more," gaining opportunities to release greed or fear, and so on.

Spend some time feeling truly grateful for *all aspects* of this situation, relationship, etc. All these aspects together create your complete knowingness and comprehension, and they also help you more clearly understand your relationship to the essence of the entire situation or relationship. You have learned to define your own boundaries, and the extremes are no longer necessary. Be at peace with all aspects of it. Be fully present in the "now" with it. Engage your "wise observer" self to see your human or emotional aspects (or someone else's) with compassion.

Practice gratitude every day—being thankful for catching a glimpse of a rainbow after a rainstorm, watching a child laugh, or being able to help an elderly person cross the street. Be grateful you can inspire hope in someone who is feeling desperate and hopeless with your kind words or actions. Moreover, now that you are grateful that you *can* inspire hope in someone else, go ahead and *do* it!

Affirmation for the Law of Gratitude

Speak this affirmation aloud slowly and deliberately from your heart with feeling: "I am grateful for this moment of this day. I am willing to receive the blessings that my gratitude invites. I am grateful for this opportunity to see my world with new eyes."

Repeat this at least nine times—three times each for your body, your mind, and your spirit. You may repeat this as many times throughout the day as you like. Take five to ten minutes to set a great tone for your daily activities.

We recommend that you use your affirmation with the associated Stone Play crystal layout on the following page, which will enhance your affirmation experience for the law of gratitude.

This Stone Play layout creates the frequency or energy of gratitude. Sit on a chair over it, lie on a table above it, or sit near it. Be in a quiet, receptive space to experience that frequency. Allow it to vibrate cellular memory or structure to open you up to more lightness of being.

Pay attention to subtle body sensations, images, or thoughts that come up.

Stone Play Crystal Layout
for the Law of Gratitude

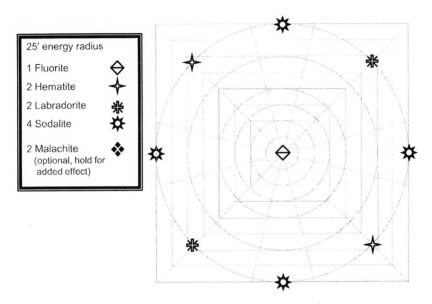

25' energy radius

1 Fluorite

2 Hematite

2 Labradorite

4 Sodalite

2 Malachite
(optional, hold for
added effect)

© 2012 The Way to Balance, LLC

THE LAW
OF GRACE

Every day, God gives us the sun—and also one moment in which we have the ability to change everything that makes us unhappy. Every day, we try to pretend that we haven't perceived that moment, that it doesn't exist—that today is the same as yesterday and will be the same as tomorrow. But if people really pay attention to their everyday lives, they will discover that magic moment. It may arrive in the instant we are doing something mundane, like putting our front-door key in the lock; it may be hidden in the quiet that follows the lunch hour or in the thousand and one things that all seem the same to us. But that moment exists—a moment when all the power of the stars becomes a part of us and enables us to perform miracles.
—Paulo Coelho, *By the River Piedra I Sat Down and Wept*

Artist: Alyssa Couture. © 2012 The Way to Balance, LLC

Chapter 10

The Law of Grace

This law allows pure love and miracles to happen. The *purity* of our thoughts and deeds allows *grace*. It is not necessarily the result of good works or positive karma. It is because, "Grace happens," like the bumper sticker says. Universal love and law, God, the Divine, One Source, whatever name you choose, grants this *just because* he loves us unconditionally. We activate this potential every time we act and decide from our sacred hearts.

What is the sacred heart? It is a magnetic vortex space within us located behind the physical heart, slightly closer to the center of the body, either a little above or a little below the physical heart. Some call this the divine flame, inner wisdom, or the home of the higher self or the soul. This is where the deepest essence of you connects with the divine. This aspect of you is your wise observer, the part of you that knows truth, love, and grace. Yet you may have covered it up with a pile of laundry and forgotten all about it.

When we are able to be fully present in a state of permitting and allowing truth, love, and grace to manifest, we begin the practice of discernment. Discernment is true, accurate wisdom marked by deep understanding, insight, and the capacity for sound judgment.

With practice and experience, discernment becomes an acquired ability that allows us to connect with God and divine wisdom on a personal level. In this state, you absolutely know truth—beyond your personality, intellectual knowledge, or experiences. At this level, you so deeply *know and live* the law of divine oneness that you engage the law of grace. Answers and experiences totally outside your realm of intellectual knowledge become available, and miracles may happen.

When we believe we are *unworthy* of love and grace, we actually block grace from blessing us. Think of grace as sunshine, undiscriminating to all who are willing to step out of the shade and into the light. Sunshine is unable to shine directly on you when you are beneath a big shade tree or inside a building without windows.

Ironically, if we think that *God owes us* for good works, then we have expectations and agendas. When we have agendas, we are not practicing discernment. Nor are we living the law of grace. We have slipped back into the law of cause and effect (karma). This expectation can block grace from happening to us.

The law of grace is perhaps better appreciated as the space for allowing/permitting miracles to occur. A recent news story on television told of a woman who was declared clinically dead following a complication from surgery. Despite heroic medical efforts to revive her for more than thirty minutes, doctors could not resuscitate her. She registered no brain activity or any other signs of life. Her family prayed intensely for her healing from the moment they learned of the complication. When the saddened medical team came out to announce she had not survived, the nurses began the necessary preparations for the body's removal. Suddenly, they heard a gasp and some coughing. The law of grace had intervened, and she came back to life with absolutely no brain damage or other signs of injury from blood and oxygen deprivation. Even the doctors interviewed described it as a miracle. This was grace at work.

In the course of our days, many smaller things happen to us that manifest themselves as the result of grace. I was in the supermarket the other day, awaiting my turn to tear off a produce bag for my vegetables. As the woman took her bag and began filling it, I gently said, "Excuse me." I expected her to shift her position so I could get my own bag. She did not respond. She silently and slowly stopped bagging, reached for a bag, and tore it off. She handed it to me with a smile. I smiled back. Our eyes met for a moment as I said, "Thank you." This small act of grace could have been easy to miss or even destroy. During the seemingly long unresponsive time after my "excuse me," perhaps I could have become annoyed or even believed she was trying to block me from getting the choice vegetables before her. Let us suppose that I felt that or assumed that and then said something nasty to her. The scene would have ended quite differently.

Healing is God's grace in action. A client named Jerry came into our healing center with very painful bone spurs on both feet. Aaron and I performed a joint healing session on him and invited God's grace and healing to flow through us. The bone spurs softened and were gone within the hour. Jerry excitedly ran up and down the stairs several times, rejoicing that his feet were pain-free.

Another example of grace as healing is when my mother developed melanoma. Aaron, my father, and I joined hands, surrounded my mother, and asked for grace to intercede. When my mother returned to the doctor, he could no longer find the cancer.

Dorothy arrived at our center and told Aaron that X-rays showed a piece of her anklebone had broken off and was floating in the area of the break. Doctors had insisted that surgical pins were necessary to repair it. However, Dorothy refused and asked Aaron if he could help her avoid the surgery. Aaron did a few healing sessions on her ankle. Several months passed, and Dorothy returned with her before and after X-rays in hand. Then she showed us how the bone fragment had reattached and mended itself as if it were never broken.

At other times, grace is about God calling people home. My elderly aunt Amanda was having difficulty breathing, and I knew she was in the process of dying. I invited her to look into my eyes as I focused on love, peace, and grace radiating from my eyes into hers. She told me, "I feel so much more peaceful, and I can breathe easier when I look into your eyes." I told her that she could look into my eyes whenever she wanted to. She looked into my eyes frequently over the next thirty-six hours. Grace inspired the words I spoke to her throughout this time. Aunt Amanda closed her eyes much of the time as I spoke to her during her last few hours. She suddenly opened her eyes again and looked straight into mine. Her eyes sparkled. She winked at me, and she passed away peacefully. This was God's precious gift of grace to both of us.

When Aaron and I have long drives ahead of us, we often get up and start driving at 2:30 a.m. The roads are spacious and peaceful. There are only the truckers and us, illuminated by stars and the moon. One night, we were driving behind two trucks for quite a distance. We decided to pull out and pass. As soon as we changed lanes, one of the truckers pulled in front of us, blocking us from passing, as he was now side by side with the other trucker. We retreated to our lane. This happened two more times precisely the same way with the same two truckers. After the third time, we accepted that there was a reason and simply drove along in a three-vehicle caravan. The sky began to turn that beautiful twilight color before daybreak. We passed by several speed traps. We smiled and turned to each other and said aloud, "Thank you, brother truckers." A short time later, we pulled into the passing lane and hesitated, waiting for a sign. They gave us a clear shot, so we passed the two truckers. All three of us honked and waved as our salute to the fellowship of the twilight hours. What a great time to travel.

Exercise for the Law of Grace

Grace is not something you acquire. Grace is given freely to all who are willing to receive it. It is like a surprise gift.

How many times in the last month were you offered grace but were not ready to receive it? Perhaps your boss suggested that you leave work early to enjoy a beautiful spring day. However, you declined and stayed at work late anyway. Maybe someone offered you an all-expense-paid trip to be his or her travel companion, and you declined.

How many times in the last month has grace beamed you and you graciously accepted? Perhaps the act of grace was something big, or perhaps it was something small. Did someone ahead of you pay your tollbooth fee? On a day when you were particularly tired or stressed, did a professional cancel a meeting and gift you some breathing room?

How many times in the last month have you practiced "random acts of senseless kindness"? Did you buy coffee for the person behind you in line? Did you gift someone something just because it felt right to gift it?

The beautiful thing about the law of grace is that it is quite contagious and it is easy to start spreading it around. Have fun, grace someone who least expects it, and expect nothing back in return.

Affirmation for the Law of Grace

Speak this affirmation aloud slowly and deliberately from your heart with feeling: "I am willing to accept grace. I live a grace-filled life, I am grateful that God's gifts manifest for my highest good."

Repeat this at least nine times—three times each for your body, your mind, and your spirit. You may repeat this as many times throughout the day as you like. Take five to ten minutes to set a great tone for your daily activities.

We recommend that you use your affirmation with the associated Stone Play crystal layout on the following page, which will enhance your affirmation experience for the law of grace.

This Stone Play layout creates the frequency or energy of God's grace. Sit on a chair over it, lie on a table above it, or sit near it. Be in a quiet, receptive space to experience that frequency. Allow it to vibrate cellular memory or structure to open you up to more lightness of being.

Pay attention to subtle body sensations, images, or thoughts that come up.

Stone Play Crystal Layout
for the Law of Grace

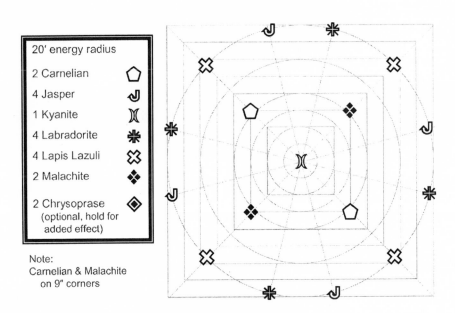

20' energy radius	
2 Carnelian	⬠
4 Jasper	⌡
1 Kyanite	)(
4 Labradorite	✳
4 Lapis Lazuli	✖
2 Malachite	❖
2 Chrysoprase (optional, hold for added effect)	◈

Note:
Carnelian & Malachite
on 9" corners

© *2012 The Way to Balance, LLC*

ARCHITECTS, INFRASTRUCTURE SPECIALISTS, AND BUILDERS

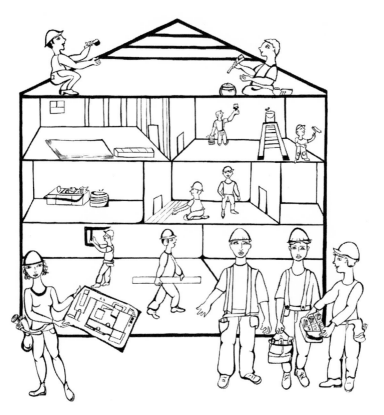

Artist: Alyssa Couture. © 2012 The Way to Balance, LLC

Chapter 11

Architects, Infrastructure Specialists, and Builders

Let us return to our metaphor from chapter 1, and imagine that the universal laws represent a team of professionals working on a building project. In this metaphor, some of these laws are *architects with blueprints,* and some are reliable *builders/carpenters* who carry out the architectural plan. Others are *infrastructure specialists* who provide electricity, heat, water, and telecommunications conduits and pathways (e.g., plumbers, electricians, etc.).

We now define these three categories of jobs more completely, staying with the metaphor of building a home.

Architects

Architects create, design, and develop the plans for buildings or structures. An architectural blueprint is the printed plan or guide the architect creates to help with the schematics. The blueprint provides the specifications, design details, plan of action, and the policies to build the structure. Without the architect's blueprint, a building may be unstable, weak, crooked, or unsatisfactory, and it may not meet the expectations and needs of the inhabitants. The builders and infrastructure specialists rely on an excellent blueprint to incorporate their important structures and systems in the appropriate locations.

Who are the architects in your life? The creators of your master plan are the law of divine oneness, the law of unconditional love, and the law of grace.

Infrastructure Specialists

These specialists include electricians, plumbers, and telecommunications technicians. Through their systems, the building has light, heat, water, sewage disposal, power for various appliances, telephone, television, and Internet access. Think of these workers as those who can provide you with the conduits and framework for the flow throughout the household. The architect relies on the specialists to install the proper systems according to the blueprint.

Who are the infrastructure specialists in your life? They are the law of universal abundance, the law of ideals, and the law of polarity/balance.

Builders and Carpenters

The builders construct the foundation, frame, walls, roof, stairways, and doorways. The builders and/or carpenters also insulate, create internal rooms, and install windows and floors. The architect relies on the builders and carpenters to build the proper design as drawn in the blueprint. The infrastructure specialists rely on them to create the space and support for their pipes, wires, cables, and so on. They also rely on the builders to provide them with sufficient time to install these systems *before* the builders and carpenters close in and finish the walls, floors, and ceilings.

Who are the builders and carpenters in your life? They are the law of cause and effect, the law of attraction, and the law of gratitude.

All Are Part of the Team!

When you are building a house you love or a life you love, all the team members play valuable roles. It is important to recognize the importance of each as well as their relationships to each other.

Some jobs seem to span a few categories. Does it really matter which job category each one fits in to? Frankly, it does not. Therefore, try not to spend a lot of time figuring out *why* we placed each job in a given category. It was actually an exercise to help stimulate you working with both sides of your brain. This process assists with the law of polarity.

It is far more important and fun to begin living and applying the concepts of all these powerful universal laws than it is to be overly (and perhaps unnecessarily) analytical.

Other Tools Needed
by the Construction Team

Artist: Alyssa Couture. © 2012 The Way to Balance, LLC

Chapter 12

Other Tools Needed by the Construction Team

Our own journeys have led us to the conclusion that these nine universal laws are just that—nine rules of the game that are important to know in order to create a life you love. The speed limit is essentially the law, whether you read the speed limit sign or not. If you go above the speed limit, the checks and balances eventually catch up to you, and a correction takes place (a ticket). Once you understand and work in harmony with the nine universal laws, life and decision-making become simpler.

Some may believe there are more than nine universal laws. In our experience, we feel a longer list of laws is redundant of the nine, a listing simply reworded or one naming supportive traits as laws.

There are human traits or characteristics that create a foundation for us to live in harmony with these universal laws. These qualities include the following:

- **Aspiration to a higher power** is a belief in some greater intelligence or plan. When we aspire to improve ourselves and be more like our Creator, we embrace change as part of the greater good. When we aspire to be more like a higher intelligence, we have standards of quality and excellence that we begin to engage. This trait particularly supports the laws of divine oneness, unconditional love, ideals, grace, and polarity.
- **Charity** is a willingness to share. When we are willing to help others by sharing what we have or what we know, we are enhancing the energy flow in the universe. This behavior

supports the laws of abundance, polarity, gratitude, cause and effect, and attraction.

- **Compassion** is the ability to *hold space* in a supportive yet detached manner for someone or for a situation. Compassion is often confused with pity or sympathy. It is more of a willingness to observe and listen with kindness *without* trying to fix or take on responsibility. Frequently, to learn compassion, we begin with empathy, wherein we become sensitive to others' thoughts and feelings. Yet empathy can turn into empathic behavior—so sensitized to others that we feel their pain or issues as our own. Being empathic is not a healthy goal, but it may be a stepping-stone to the goal of compassion. This quality of compassion is extremely important to support the laws of unconditional love, divine oneness, cause and effect, ideals, attraction, and polarity.

- **Humility** means letting go of ego or self-centeredness; it is a trait of modesty or respectfulness. It is having an unassuming, humble nature, making a right estimate of one's self. Humility is a foundation for the laws of unconditional love, cause and effect, polarity and grace.

- **Courage** means choosing to act without being held back by fear. It is an ability to face danger, difficulty, uncertainty, or pain without being overcome by fear or without being deflected from a chosen course of action. Courage shows strength and fortitude, without denying the existence of fear. Courage promotes the laws of cause and effect, ideals, abundance, and gratitude.

- **Dedication** means being devoted or committed to something, setting something aside for a purpose. It is a capacity to stay focused on a goal or ideal. Dedication is necessary for the laws of divine oneness, ideals, attraction, and gratitude.

- **Faith** is a conviction for, devotion to, or trust in someone or something without demanding logical proof. It means to be true to a strongly held set of principles or beliefs. Faith is an underlayment for the laws of divine oneness, unconditional love, ideals, attraction, abundance, and grace.

- **Forgiveness** is an act of pardoning oneself or somebody else for a mistake or wrongdoing. Forgiveness allows room for imperfection or weakness in oneself and others. The International Forgiveness Institute defines forgiveness as a response to an injustice (a moral wrong). It is a turning to the *good* in the face of this wrongdoing. Forgiveness is the foregoing of resentment or revenge when the wrongdoer's actions deserve it and giving the gifts of mercy, generosity, and love when the wrongdoer does not deserve them. It is equally important to know what forgiveness is *not*. It is *not* forgetting, denying, condoning, excusing, condemning, forgiving with a sense of moral superiority, or seeking justice or compensation (Enright, 2012). *As we give the gift of forgiveness, we heal ourselves.* Forgiveness is a foundation for the laws of divine oneness, unconditional love, cause and effect, attraction, and grace.

- **Contemplation** means applying the mind or intuition to reason, reflect, meditate, or consider in order to gain insights, knowledge, or awareness. It is calm and careful thought, a capacity to notice, realize, or learn something because you take the time to observe and reflect. It is very important to contemplate before you make decisions or form opinions. Contemplation helps expand our understanding, open-mindedness, and awareness. Without it, we may be ignorant, narrow-minded, judgmental, and unaware. Contemplation supports the laws of divine oneness, unconditional love, ideals, attraction, and gratitude.

- **Generosity** is a kind or noble trait of character; a willingness to share, to give money, to provide help or time freely to others. Generosity creates a foundation for the laws of attraction, abundance, and grace.

- **Honesty** is the quality, condition, or characteristic of being fair, truthful, sincere, and morally upright. Honesty is an underlayment for the laws of cause and effect, ideals, attraction, polarity, and abundance.

- **Hope** is defined as a wish for something to happen or to be true, especially feeling that something desirable is likely to happen or is possible. Hope engages a feeling of trust, opportunity, potential, and imagination. Hope helps engage the laws of divine oneness, unconditional love, ideals, attraction, abundance, and grace.

- **Joy** is the emotion evoked by a sense of well-being, great happiness, and appreciation, especially of a spiritual kind. In this sense, *joy is an inside job*, as true joy is not contingent upon outside conditions or people. It is inner contentment, regardless of what circumstances are with you or those around you. Joy supports the laws of divine oneness, gratitude, and grace.
- **Leadership** means the ability to guide, direct, or influence people in a constructive manner. The best way of demonstrating leadership is by being an example for others to aspire to by incorporating the universal laws and supportive traits into your daily life. Leadership invokes the laws of unconditional love, ideals, attraction, polarity, and grace.
- **Patience** is the capacity for waiting without becoming annoyed or upset, to persevere calmly when faced with difficulties. It is not hasty or impetuous. It is related to the virtues or habits of inner strength, serenity, and self-control. Patience is a foundation for the laws of cause and effect, ideals, attraction, abundance, and grace.
- **Discernment** is true, accurate wisdom marked by deep understanding, insight, and the capacity for sound judgment. With the process of discernment, you also access universal truth and knowledge outside your intellect or personality. With practice, discernment becomes your direct connection with God from within you. At this level, you so deeply *know and live* the law of divine oneness that you engage all the laws, especially the law of grace.

RISE ABOVE
CHALLENGES

Artist: Alyssa Couture. © 2012 The Way to Balance, LLC

Chapter 13

Rise above Challenges

As you read in the introduction to this book, I personally know about duress, challenges, and juggling multiple priorities. I learned to incorporate the knowledge I gained from my near-death experience and what I discovered from my own and clients' experiences in order to rise above apparent obstacles. I have come to realize people face common challenges when they are trying to manifest better things in their lives.

Challenges to Successful Manifestations

There are typical obstacles that Aaron and I have either observed among our clients and students or lived through ourselves. We summarize them below and offer suggestions to rise above them.

Doubt: You may doubt that you can accomplish your goals, and not trust yourself to apply the laws correctly. This can be a result of perfectionistic tendencies, unrealistic goals, or unworthiness. Here's a suggestion: Try it anyway. When you first learned to ride a bike or drive a car, you were wobbly and had a few mishaps. Yet, your consistent practice helped you become better. In addition, setting goals or ideals that are the polar opposite of your current situation may be hard for you to believe. For example, if you are barely able to pay your rent each month, you may have a hard time consistently believing you will own a multimillion-dollar oceanfront home. Therefore, consider some interim short-term goals, such as acquiring new work at better pay or first owning a condominium.

Unworthiness: You may feel that you do not deserve what you desire. This can include self-loathing or believing you do not even deserve to exist. Unworthiness is frequently associated with attachment to stories and self-sabotage. Here's a suggestion: Review the laws of unconditional love, gratitude, and grace. Imagine that the unconditional love for a puppy or young baby is really for you. The loving puppy or baby is your reflection back at you for being the love that you are. Reflect or consider *where* your story or belief that you are unworthy *came from*. Perhaps it was something someone said or did long ago. However, is it really true? Is it possible that it was always untrue, that this person was incorrect? Is it possible that it is no longer true for you at this point in your life? What is true for your parents or siblings or spouse may not be at all true for *you*. Imagine how you might feel without attaching to your past stories or the stories of others about you.

Self-sabotage: You may have a conscious or unconscious desire to keep the status quo and to reject change. At times, this relates to a fear of success, a fear of failure, or an attachment to stories. Self-sabotage may indicate you like your life exactly as it is. Here's a suggestion: It is very helpful to follow this impulse to the place where the self-sabotage began. Does it relate more to attachment to stories, fear of success, fear of failure, or something else? Once you have a better sense of what else this feeling involves, work on it from those approaches.

Attachment to stories about who and what you are: An attachment to stories includes both your self-talk within yourself and your belief in what others have told you. Others may verbally tell you or suggest these stories to you by how they treat your personhood and ideas with disrespect. It is a form of victimhood. Here's a suggestion: It is very helpful to recognize that as humans, we often entangle *facts/*history with our *stories/*interpretation of the facts. Example, I needed to disentangle the *fact* that a neighbor sexually molested me from any *interpretation* of it. Saying that I am a victim or that he is evil is what we call the *story*. As I began to live in harmony with the laws, I became grateful for the variety of experiences in my life that helped me become the humble healer and teacher that I am today. Without some variety, perhaps I would have been egocentric, and I might not have been able to truthfully say, "I know how you feel. I understand," to the wounded clients who came to me to heal. *If I can do it, you can do it.* I can offer students/clients hope and possibilities *because* of my history and how I rose above my challenges.

Victimhood: This challenge is an attachment to your stories. In your story, you believe that something or someone outside yourself must change before you can accomplish your goal. Victimhood is disempowerment, and you then feel that you cannot change unless someone else behaves differently. Here's a suggestion: If you are currently threatened, victimized, or belittled, then immediately seek professional assistance from therapists, shelters, law enforcement, or other appropriate resources. It took me enduring years of verbal abuse in a long-term relationship with a violent partner before I realized it was indeed abuse. It was not until he choked me that I sought outside help and learned that I deserved better. If your victim consciousness relates to something that happened to you long ago that is not an active threat in your life today, try to disentangle the story from the historical facts.

Fear of success: This fear frequently relates to unworthiness or an actual fear that success will change you so much that you will become a stranger to yourself. People sometimes equate success with behaviors they dislike in successful people they have met or heard of. You may even know some wealthy people who are self-centered or greedy. Here's a suggestion: It is very important to learn how to separate your *definition* of success from the *behaviors* of individuals who are successful. You can choose how *you behave* as a successful person versus what you observe in others whom you do not admire. You are the creator of your own choices.

Fear of failure: This fear can be very paralyzing for people. It often results from people believing that someone will stop loving them if they make a mistake. It may also mean they will not love themselves if they are less than perfect. Here's a suggestion: It is helpful to follow through in your imagination a few steps. For example, if you are interested in applying for a new job and you are afraid that you may fail to get the job, ask yourself, "What is the *worst* thing that can happen if I do not get this new job?" Perhaps you will stay in your current job longer. On the other hand, if you are unemployed, not getting the job may mean that you could lose your house. But is it actually true that you will lose your house based on this particular job interview? If yes, then what is the worst that can happen? Will you be homeless? Alternatively, do you have friends and family who will let you stay with them for a while? Sometimes walking yourself through the scenarios a bit can take away the fear.

One of our clients lost his job as an artist in the entertainment industry because of cutbacks. He held on until he could no longer afford housing. He then moved in with family and friends for a while. As his unemployment period grew longer, he realized he could not stay longer in any of his temporary situations. He packed his remaining belongings into his car, and he lived there for an extended period. Friends allowed him to come and shower weekly and spend a night or two when it was bitterly cold outside, but he mostly lived in his car all winter long.

When he eventually got a new job and found a new place to live, we talked to him about how he felt during the process, especially upon reflection, knowing what he knew now. He realized how strong, innovative, and resilient he had become through the journey. It was very unpleasant at times, but he has a newfound appreciation for the simplest of comforts and pleasures in life. He healed his fear of *the worst-case scenario* by living through it.

Inflexibility: Many are too rigid in their approach and stay fixated on precisely how their goals must manifest or what they must look like. Inflexibility also prevents you from going with the flow, especially in regard to changes in schedules, life circumstances, and more. Inflexibility or rigidity causes you to reject your granted gifts just as the man in the flood rejected God's rescue via human helpers in chapter 6. Here's a suggestion: Keep your intention simple without over-defining details. Be open to all the possibilities that can contribute to your highest good. Some of Aaron's and my amazing adventures have been a result of *accidentally* taking a *wrong* turn on roads when we were out driving somewhere. We try to stay open to the universe's plan for us to be where we find ourselves, even if that's many miles from where we thought we were going!

Conflicts: Conflicts between your stated goal and your thoughts and actions cancel manifestation. Here's a suggestion: If your stated goal or ideal is more tranquility in your life, then it is important to choose activities and thoughts that support that. Learn to detach from your phone, e-mail, or social media. Responding to those constant interruptions cancels your desire for tranquility. Simply check messages at intervals that are convenient to you rather than immediately grabbing the phone each time a text or call comes in.

Superheroes: These people attempt to do it all themselves and reject outside help. The first type of superhero is overly responsible, controlling, or inflexible. The second type of superhero requires a certain level of quality. Delegating certain jobs to others may yield results of a lesser quality if they are not delegated to the appropriate people. For example, asking someone with no bookkeeping skills to perform bookkeeping duties would include concerns about the quality of that person's work. Here's a suggestion: Determine which type of superhero you are. If you are the first type, learn to delegate simpler tasks and let go of how it is done. A client complained that her husband never helped her with household chores. He told me that she was never satisfied with how he performed the tasks at home, so he stopped trying. I assigned homework to them. She needed to ask him to change the bedding in their room and their children's rooms. At her next appointment, I asked how it went. She complained that he did it all wrong and that she had to do it all over again, which caused an argument. I asked her to clarify, and it turned out that she disapproved of how he tucked the sheets at the bottom of the mattress and how he positioned the top sheet on the bed. I asked her how important that was to her in terms of the health and well-being of the family. It certainly was not a life or death crisis, yet she fixated on it. I encouraged her to recognize how much of her energy such a simple thing had consumed. I asked if they had tried doing the bedding together the first time so that her technique would be clear to her husband. Her surprised look confirmed that she had not considered that. The problem resolved itself after they went home and they changed the bedding together once. Now she can delegate new tasks, and he is happy to help when she does not criticize his technique.

Normally, the second type of superhero concern (quality) is resolved in the same way.

We sometimes wonder how many household arguments take place over which way the toilet paper roll hangs (over or under). How important is that to you? Can you let it go? (If not, we did recently see a reversible toilet paper mount in a catalog. It simply rotates for each user.)

In business situations, the second type of superhero may have valid quality concerns about delegation. It may mean that you need to delegate to someone different. Not everyone has the same skill set. We will cover more about finding help in the next section.

Impatience: This typically relates to control issues or a need for instant gratification. Here's a suggestion: Refer to the superhero discussion above. Remember, as we covered in chapter 7, "The Law of Polarity (Balance)," successful manifestation requires both masculine (action) and feminine (allowing) energies. Even following conception, we allow time for the embryo to develop into a baby.

"Issues in your tissues": This idea relates to unconscious conflicts between what you desire and what messages your body sends out. This is about healing unresolved cellular memory in your body. We covered this in chapter 6, "The Law of Attraction (Manifestation)," which included my personal example of cellular memory from sexual abuse and rape. Here's a suggestion: Seek holistic practitioners or healing tools that specifically work on cellular memory. Somatoemotional release is one modality that assists in this process. In our healing center, all of us use our own version of somatoemotional techniques, including frequency-matching techniques to dislodge cellular memory. Clients and students frequently work at home with our sound therapy series and aromatherapies, which mimic the frequencies of various emotional patterns and thus promote more rapid healing and releases from the cellular memory of the body, not to mention the rewiring of the brain.

"Hardwired to your history": This idea relates to the attachment you have to your stories as well as what we refer to as "neuronal entanglements." The brain literally lights up and goes into autopilot mode in the midst of certain triggers. The neuronal pathways are stuck in this mode until the pattern releases from the brain. Here's a suggestion: This problem is very similar to "issues in your tissues." Other techniques include hypnotherapy, emotional freedom technique, and certain specialized forms of acupressure.

Lack of focus or commitment: This is often a result of misplaced priorities. Here's a suggestion: Ask yourself, "Am I satisfied with my life exactly as it is?" If not, then select *one* priority that would increase your life satisfaction instead of trying to change everything at once. Establish your ideal(s) as suggested in chapter 5, "The Law of Ideals." If the majority of your daily activities and thoughts are not in harmony with your ideals, then eliminate as many activities that are in conflict with them as possible. Frequently, clients complain to us about how their jobs do not support their ideals. Is that true? During the years that I was both a banker and a healer, I tried to be the most spiritual banker I could be. I applied my life ideals to how I approached my job, which changed my attitude and how I accomplished my work. I became more efficient at everything I did and recognized that the banking job served as a very valuable stepping-stone. Not only did it pay our healing center bills until we were established, but I also learned many skills applicable to owning our own business.

Chapter 14

Live with Joy and Grace

*God grant me the serenity
to accept the people I cannot change,
the courage to change the one I can,
and the wisdom to know it is* me.
—Author unknown, *Serenity Prayer Redux*

Now you know how the nine universal laws work together as a construction team. You begin to work in harmony with them to create a life filled with joy and grace. You recognize that you are not a victim of circumstances and that joy and inner peace are an inside job. You are no longer subject to the will of others. You do not need to suffer the ebb and flow of the ocean waves. You remember to ride your surfboard, even if it seems like you're riding a tsunami.

Other Suggestions

- As we recommended at the beginning of the book, read the entire book once through and then spend two to four weeks per chapter on your second pass-through.
- Continue to use the daily affirmations and Stone Play crystal layouts even when you are not reading the book. Pick the affirmations you feel you need the most help with and use them daily for forty-five days.
- If you feel stuck, revisit chapter 13, "Rise above Challenges," or pick a law chapter to revisit.
- Simplify your priorities and eliminate lesser priorities or move them to a back burner. I tend to use a lettering system of A,

B, and C. It is important to remember that not everything can be an A or a B.

- Be flexible about shifting priorities if one is truly urgent (such as my family's health crises and deaths). Otherwise, be true to the ideals you established in chapter 5 and maintain activities that support those ideals. Learn to say, "No, thank you," to activities that do not support your ideals.

- Engage helpers. You may literally ask family, friends, or volunteers to help you with chores and projects. You can choose not to be a superhero.

- Engage the angelic realm to help you with absolutely anything and everything. Yes, there are angels who specialize in automobiles, marketing, lost objects, and more. I recently called upon strong angels to help with our camper septic, and they helped me pull a stuck valve underneath our camper. I also requested an angel to help me find a new car when my old one died. That particular adventure was quite funny, as this tough-looking angel called himself Armand. I asked him why he thought he could help me, and he replied, "I was the best car dealer you'd ever meet when I was human. I am even better from the other side." Sure enough, I found my car within forty-eight hours. Jean Slatter wrote a wonderful book titled *Hiring the Heavens* (2005) about engaging angelic helpers. That book also served as a gentle reminder for me at this time.

- Keep a sense of humor and take yourself more lightly. We like to do silly things that create belly laughs—those big body-shaking bouts of laughter that sometimes bring tears to your eyes. This action actually changes the biochemistry in your brain, promotes a sense of well-being, and boosts your immune system. It helps to be more childlike (not to be confused with childish). I had a particularly good belly laugh at work when a very slender young client's pants were a little large on her and they kept slipping down. I joked with her and said, "You need some more spaghetti to fill up those pants." She looked at me, laughed, and said, "You are so silly. I can't do that. My mother would yell at me if I poured a pan of spaghetti and meatballs down my pants!"

- Create some inactivity time for yourself each day, even if it is as short as fifteen minutes. Ideally, you can meditate, pray, write poetry, listen to inspiring music, or soak in the tub during this time. Alternatively, you can simply practice letting yourself do absolutely nothing but *be*.
- It is best to have an hour for engaging the *feminine* incubation time daily, but you should start with what you can do. Remember, the *masculine* energy is action and activity, and the *feminine* energy is magnetic—attracting and creating space to realize your dreams. *Action* and *space* work together. They co-create your goals.

Parting Thoughts

It has been a joy to impart our understanding of the *Nine Simple Laws to Create Joy and Grace*. Both of us have truly had fun writing, sharing stories and exercises to help you manifest joy and grace in your life.

Aaron and I also wrote "A Prayer for Love and Miracles," which appears on the following page. We feel it helps us to stay open to possibilities and remain full of gratitude. The prayer serves as a complement to incorporate the laws into our daily lives.

We dream of a world where joy and peace reign as we all apply God's nine universal laws. Our vision is that everyone recognizes that we are not separate, we are all one. Our common core human DNA is the adamantine particle, also known as divine love, which empowers us to transform our thoughts into reality. May you choose to spread your joy and grace with those you meet on your journey. Happy manifesting!

A Prayer for Love and Miracles

I call upon the purest love and light of Father-Mother God,
the one source of all,
and the Christ consciousness,
to surround me and fill me with the greatest love,
compassion, and joy.

I choose the law of grace that invites the purity of God's love and
miracles on earth.

I ask that this love and grace open the hearts and minds of all earth's
inhabitants to world peace and the oneness of all.

I ask for healing love and miracles for myself, for mother earth, and
for all my brothers and sisters in the human, animal, plant, and
mineral kingdoms and the spiritual realms.

I am love.
I am love.
I am love.

I am.
I am.
I am.
And so it is—
Amen.

Stone Play Crystal Legend

- ✸ Amethyst - 4
- ✗ Angelite/Anhydrite - 2
- ⌘ Blue Lace Agate - 2
- ⬠ Carnelian - 4
- ♡ Chalcedony - 4
- ◈ Chrysoprase - 2
- ✾ Citrine - 5
- ▲ Emerald - 4
- ⬖ Fluorite - 1
- ✳ Garnet - 4
- ✛ Hematite - 2
- ♪ Jasper - 4

- ✇ Kyanite - 4
- ✳ Labradorite - 4
- ✕ Lapis Lazuli - 1
- ❖ Malachite - 6
- ☾ Mookaite - 8
- ⊘ Moonstone - 8
- ▣ Rhodonite - 4
- ✴ Rose Quartz - 4
- ♋ Ruby Zoisite - 4
- ▱ Selenite - 4
- ◇ Serpentine - 4
- ✸ Sodalite - 4

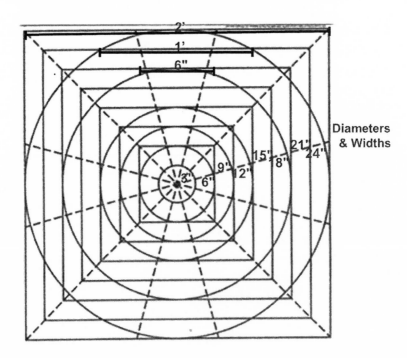

Diameters & Widths

© 2012 The Way to Balance, LLC

References

Beatles. 1968. "Revolution 9." *The White Album*. London: Apple Records.

Bro, Harmon Hartzell, PhD. *A Seer Out of Season: The Life of Edgar Cayce*. New York: New American Library, a division of Penguin Books USA Inc., 1989.

Chung, Andrew. "Odds are next U.S. president will be left-handed." *Toronto Star*, March 2, 2008.

Coelho, Paulo. *By the River Piedra I Sat Down and Wept: A Novel of Forgiveness*. New York: HarperCollins Publishers, Inc., 1996.

Gibran, Kahlil. *The Prophet*. Oxford: OneWorld Publications, 1998.

Green, Glenda. *Love without End: Jesus Speaks*. Sedona, AZ: Spiritis Publishing, 1999.

Hawkins, David R., MD, PhD. *Power vs. Force: The Hidden Determinants of Human Behavior*. Carlsbad, CA: Hay House, Inc., 1998.

Hicks, Esther and Jerry. *The Law of Attraction: The Basics of the Teachings of Abraham*. Carlsbad, CA: Hay House, Inc., 2006.

Hicks, Esther and Jerry, and Wayne W. Dyer. *Ask and It Is Given: Learning to Manifest Your Desires*. Carlsbad, CA: Hay House, Inc., 2004.

Lao-tzu. *Tao Te Ching*. Translated by Stephen Mitchell. New York: HarperCollins Publishers, Inc., 1988.

Lipton, Bruce H., PhD. *The Biology of Belief: Unleashing the Power of Consciousness, Matter & Miracles*. Carlsbad, CA: Hay House, Inc., 2008.

Northrup, Christiane, MD. *Women's Bodies, Women's Wisdom: Creating Physical and Emotional Health and Healing*. New York: Random House, Inc., 2010.

Rotstein, Gary. "Another left-handed president? It's looking that way." *Pittsburgh Post-Gazette*, February 25, 2008.

Shri Krishna. *Bhagavad Gita*. Translated by Stephen Mitchell. New York: Random House, Inc., 2000.

Slatter, Jean. *Hiring the Heavens*. Novato, CA: New World Library, 2005.

Webster's Encyclopedic Unabridged Dictionary of the English Language. San Diego, CA: Thunder Bay Press, 2001.

Enright, Robert. "What Is Forgiveness?" *International Forgiveness Institute*, http://www.internationalforgiveness.com/what-is-forgiveness/, accessed July 2012.

CPSIA information can be obtained at www.ICGtesting.com
Printed in the USA
LVOW100142070513

332586LV00001B/151/P